COOKED RAW

Published by Familius LLC, www.familius.com

Familius books are available at special discounts for bulk purchases for sales promotions, family, or corporate use. Special editions, including personalized covers, excerpts of existing books, or books with corporate logos, can be created in large quantities for special needs. For more information, contact Premium Sales at 559-876-2170 or email specialmarkets@familius.com.

Library of Congress Catalog-in-Publication Data
2014957008
pISBN 9781939629364
eISBN 9781939629975

Printed in the United States of America

Edited by Brooke Jorden
Cover and book design by David Miles
Cover photograph © Lynn Karlin

10 9 8 7 6 5 4 3 2 1

First Edition

COOKED RAW

HOW ONE CELEBRITY CHEF RISKED EVERYTHING TO CHANGE THE WAY WE EAT

MATTHEW KENNEY

MY DEEPEST APPRECIATION goes out to all who have shaped my journey over the years and to those who continue to work beside me on a daily basis. I hope that my impact on your lives will be as meaningful as yours has been on mine. This book would not be complete without success and failure, challenge and growth, alignment and resistance. For this reason, I acknowledge and appreciate you all, the friends and supporters, adversaries and naysayers, collaborators and partners, family and loved ones, and especially my colleagues, who run beside me on this journey to craft the future of food. You are all a part of this story in some way, and I thank you.

—M.K.

CONTENTS

PANCAKE BREAKFAST

Try blueberry pancakes on a chilled morning with warm, sweet, milky coffee in Styrofoam cups. They have crispy edges, slightly burnt from the heat of butter and a black skillet, overloaded with the tiny and tart wild Maine berries, and generously covered with local maple syrup. It would never occur to most of the world that men in the small towns of America would be awake at this hour, congregating over these sweet delicacies before walking through the woods for hours. The coffee goes down like water—we can easily drink three or four cups—as we slowly emerge from the morning haze.

HUNTER

"Matt, ready to go huntin'?"

I mumbled something indicating my desire to do just that, but I did not move. It was well before sunrise. My dad's soothing voice was no competition for a blistering headache, the product of a long night of cheap beer and other libations.

Ignoring my haze, Dad began to tell me about a dream he'd had in the night about the enormous buck we had seen several times in deer season over the last couple years. The buck always seemed to turn up, but we could never get close enough take a clean shot. It wasn't until my eye focused on the paper in my dad's hand that I actually considered moving from my childhood bed. It was a map he'd drawn of the deer's whereabouts, indicating precisely where and how I was going to shoot it.

I was home for a late fall weekend, taking a break from my college routine and seeing my local Maine friends. In reality, walking through the damp, dark woods with a loaded rifle fell somewhere between an ice bath and chewing glass on the excitement scale. It speaks volumes of my desire to please my father that I crawled out of bed and managed to throw on my insulated L.L. Bean boots, thick wool socks, dark green pants that weighed more than a young elephant, and the requisite red-and-black plaid coat. Full-on fluorescent orange was for the tourists, but still, staying in the confines of safety, the comically bright orange cap rounded it off. My gloves were deerskin, ironically, lined with soft inserts and broken in so that the trigger finger would not be compromised.

A thermos of coffee in hand, I grabbed our most precise weapon, a bolt-action 7mm Magnum with its high-powered Bausch and Lomb scope, and a handful of 175-grain bullets. The feel of the cold steel against my hands and the smell of its well-oiled barrel created that familiar sense of anxiety I always felt when walking into the woods, never knowing what I should expect.

My dad, Robert Kenney, explained the map during the twenty-minute ride to my grandfather's property in Brooks, a small Maine farming town. Deer tend to be habitual and often will follow the same paths, depending on the wind and terrain, but older bucks tend to be intelligent and crafty, as they've survived a few hunting seasons and their instincts are well honed. We'd seen deer literally crawling to stay low in the brush in order to evade a predator. When Dad not only pointed out the general area where we'd find this deer, but also exactly where I should shoot it, I was skeptical, to say the least. We were talking about an area that included hundreds of acres and uncountable potential escape routes. Robert Kenney can fix anything and doesn't overpromise—except when it comes to the Red Sox winning and the chances of getting a deer. So, I took it all with a grain of salt.

Hunting wasn't new to me. When I was about eight, I started trailing my dad through the woods all day while he taught me how to walk quietly, how to understand the wind, how to use a compass, and how to "smell" a deer, something he always tried to explain.

"Matt, you smell that? There's a deer around here."

We'd examine the deer droppings, critiquing the size of the pellets ("Big buck!") and the color and dryness ("This one's fresh"). Tracks were always another sign, and the real prize deer, the big ones, would use their ample antlers to scrape and mark trees, taking off a layer of bark. If you saw fresh scrapings on a tree, you knew you were in the right place.

We usually walked; that was how my dad and I liked to hunt. Other hunters sit all day, waiting, which is a good strategy if you know you're on a regular "deer crossing." Some build tree stands, which are the adult version of a treehouse. I was never into that—the Maine woods are too cold in the late fall, and it's a bore to sit in a tree all day, even with a good book. I enjoyed walking on the mixed terrain, feeling the autumn leaves crunching under my squishy boots, snapping twigs, and, at other times, creeping over mossy hills quietly.

The deep woods can be a very profound place. You might come across remnants of a building's foundation on the top of an expansive mountain or a rusty barbed wire fence, alluding to life perhaps a hundred years ago. You may see a couple squirrels chasing one another in the sun or a lone white rabbit hop along out of your way. Occasionally, while inching through thick brush, I would scare a pheasant out of its perch and, at the same time, scare myself out of my boots.

Of course, before you can even walk into the woods, you must learn gun safety and how to handle the various types of weapons. I started with BB guns. I could hit a telephone pole or a bird on a wire from well over one hundred feet away—a hobby I practiced from my second-floor bedroom window on a regular basis. I must have gone through ten thousand BBs as a child and got into some trouble because of it. My dad was just starting his business in those days, so we only had a couple of guns: a hand-me-down Winchester and an old bolt-action rig that couldn't hit a barn from ten yards away.

I got my first deer with the classic Winchester 30-30, a no-nonsense lever-action rifle—similar to the ones you see on old western TV shows—with a wooden handle and wooden armrest and the remainder cold, blue steel. I'd learned the action itself from my BB guns, which were modeled after these. I was just ten years old—the year you are allowed to hunt, supervised, in Maine—and I was about as tall as the gun. In all fairness, my first deer may have been a bit of beginner's luck, but it sure made an impression.

We had walked pretty deep into the woods on that dry and clear November afternoon. It felt like noon, but since we'd only entered the woods at daybreak, it was probably only 9 a.m. We stopped to share a Snickers bar, and my dad sipped on the lukewarm coffee in his pale green Coleman thermos. He gave me the good gun—the lever action—and he carried the bolt. Our guns were resting on a tree while we snacked and took in the quiet, cool air. I imagine it must have been such a tender moment for him, seeing his young son out there on the land he grew up around, ready to hit the family tradition head on. I loved it, too, and even at that young age, I appreciated the ceremony of the break and savored the moment.

Still, you don't expect action when you let your guard down like that, so when I saw a big buck trotting at a decent clip about a hundred yards away, it was a bit of a shock. Dad didn't see it.

"Dad, there's a deer!" I exclaimed, keeping my voice low.

"Shoot it," he immediately and instinctually responded.

I grabbed that lever action from the tree and pumped off three rounds right at the buck's antlers. It all happened so fast, I'm not sure I even raised the sights to eye level, but it felt controlled. I'd had enough experience firing my BB gun at birds and launching snowballs at friends flying down icy hills on toboggans that I knew to aim ahead a bit. In what felt like three seconds, the deer was out of sight.

"You got him, Matt!"

I didn't see a shot connect, nor did I see the deer, so I didn't understand what he meant. He started walking toward where the deer had been, and I followed, my heart pumping a hundred miles an hour.

Sure enough, that eight-point buck was flat out; my shot nailed it right above the eye.

"I'll be damned," Dad said.

We dressed the deer out, dragged it to my uncle's house, and showed off a bit, nobody really believing that the shot and kill were mine. After we got home, we took the head to Leroy Garten, the local taxidermist, who mounted it as a souvenir—one that still hangs in my parents' den today.

All these memories were—or are—poetic to me.

Years later, now a college student, I thought of that first kill as we pulled up at my Uncle Richard's house, adjacent to the area we planned to hunt. Dad showed the map to Richard and my cousin, Jim, who I'm sure wanted to believe in the plan. They drove me to an old logging road and told me to walk about half a mile to a clearing by a big apple tree and wait. The three of them planned to spread out and walk through a thickly grown hilly expanse of land until they reached a swamp. Dad's dream, a product of growing up on this land and what he claims are "Indian instincts," informed him that the deer would smell or hear them and run away, heading right to where I was standing. So I waited.

If you've ever been deep into the woods alone, you understand that sensory experiences are abundant. I still recall the aroma of wet leaves, the crackle of cold branches, and how something as minimal as the rustling of squirrels can set the heart racing. I've spent some of my best days in the woods: the fresh snow hitting my face, the late afternoon sun warming the earth to the point that I'd lie down, feeling perhaps as connected to Mother Nature as one can be. This was not one of those days, however. I was tired, hungover, and my youthful passion for hunting had been diminished by a growing sensitivity toward animals and a couple of bad shots that led to the agonizing experience of seeing an animal suffering. Still, being a hunter was in my blood, and I excelled at it.

It felt like hours, though, in reality, it was probably less than ninety minutes. I could hear my Uncle Richard crashing through the brush in the distance, so I assumed the hunt was over and no deer had been aroused. They will often just lie low in the moss, listening and watching as you walk right past them.

Then I heard the faintest snap through thick alders no more than a hundred and fifty yards in front of me. I did not raise my gun, as it could have been another hunter and nothing was in sight. A moment later, I saw that broad rack of antlers and the deer's beautiful head, eyes and ears on high alert. He paused, and, while my heart rate was accelerated, I remained calm, slowly unlocked my safety, and raised the rifle. With crosshairs firmly planted on the high end of the buck's front shoulder, I gently squeezed the trigger. The sound of a rifle shot ringing out from far away is so different from when you stand behind it. You control that power, and you learn to respect it.

The shot was clean, and the deer dropped in its tracks. Soon, we all congregated at the body of the deer in wonder at how this enigma was now in our possession. In all my years of hunting, I had never witnessed one of the "big ones" make the shot seem easy.

"I like when a plan comes together," Dad said.

So began an afternoon of dressing the animal, carrying all two hundred and twenty pounds of it out of the woods and to our truck, ready to take it home. When you shoot a deer, it's not quite as simple as firing the shot and then cooking up a filet. The process begins with the successful shot, but many variables are necessary to ensure that you end up with quality venison.

The most important thing when shooting a deer is firing a clean shot, one that will provide an immediate kill without causing the animal to suffer. A shot to the hind-quarter, for example, can ruin much of the meat, and a shot that isn't clean can just cause injury, which is both inhumane and creates stress in the animal that will impact the tenderness of the meat.

After making a clean shot and bringing the deer down, you must dress it out, which requires a very sharp hunting knife, some precise butchering skills, and a lot of patience. This has to be done while the animal is still warm, and it has to be done thoroughly or the internal organs remaining will spoil the meat. Once you make an incision, you must open up the entire belly and carefully, without puncturing anything, remove the liver, heart, intestines, and all other organs. If you puncture something, you'll be rewarded with a mess and a smell that will teach you not to make the same mistake again. Although some old, salty Maine hunters will often head back to camp and cook the liver on the spot for lunch, deer liver isn't a delicacy, and we usually left the organs for the scavengers in the woods.

With the deer dressed and in our truck, we headed to the tagging station. The protocol for reporting your catch requires that you take your deer to a licensed station to register your kill. There, a volunteer punches a hole in your license, essentially ending hunting season since Maine law allows only one deer per hunter per season. We posed for a quick picture in front of the station then headed back home.

I look back at the photo from that day with such bittersweet emotion. It was the final hunting outing of hundreds with my dad—an activity I had relished like no other. And yet, something was different. I had become more sensitive to nature. It wasn't exhilarating or satisfying to take from nature the way it had been in the past. This time, I felt I was simply going through a habitual motion, as if I was fulfilling a duty rather than sporting or providing larder for our home.

It would take me nearly twenty years to reconcile these mixed feelings.

MAINE CRABMEAT ROLL

Independent crab pickers don't pick every day. They set up an operation a couple times a week in the home kitchen; it's a family affair. The best crab meat is just-picked, sweet and fresh, with only a slight hint of the salty brine of the sea. Some love the flaky meat with mayonnaise, but it's so silken and rich with olive oil and generous amounts of pepper, packed into a warm, butter-toasted bun with a slice of tomato. Add avocado and a wedge of crisp romaine, if you'd like.

SEEKER

Every morning during my childhood, I looked out the dormer window of my second-floor bedroom at Penobscot Bay. Depending on the time of year, this rocky inlet had steam rising from its surface into the frigid air, whitecaps warning of a pending storm, or brilliant diamond sparkles offering the promise and prosperity of a sunny summer morning. Lobster boats worked their way in and out of the harbor, and larger ships lay in wait to access the cargo port on the other side of town.

Giant piles of salt were visible in the distance, a stark reminder of how much these snow- and ice-filled roads slowed down during winter in the Northeast. When you grow up in an environment that is exposed to the full force of four seasons, you automatically learn to work in sync with nature and its inherent magic.

My parents briefly lived in Connecticut, where I was born, before moving back to their native Maine to be closer to family and so my dad could start his construction business. By the time I was a year old, he had built the spacious house that I would live in until I left for college. The only thing separating us from the woods was our big backyard, and the only thing separating us from the ocean was a big field.

Searsport, Maine, is a town of about two thousand with a "downtown" that spans a couple hundred yards and has never had a stoplight. The notable business in town is the Penobscot Marine Museum, which memorializes the town's once-booming shipping business. It is a testament to the handful of sea captains' enormous homes that still exist, although most have now been converted to antique stores, bed and breakfasts, or playgrounds for real-estate hobbyists.

Overall, Searsport was a place of optimism, and the frigid Penobscot Bay seemed to offer some vision into a world of possibilities. I took it that way, at least. In fact, I'd walk on the beach even in my teens, half-believing I'd find a message in a bottle or some lost treasure that had made its way across the world to our shores. Everything seemed to move along slowly, as it should, and life was always pretty peaceful for me.

My sister, Maryellen, was two years younger, and although we had very different interests growing up, we also had a lot of common ground with our pets and activities. Much later, my brother, Patrick, would join us when I was fifteen and in high school. This new addition really lit up our household.

As I got older and certain childhood memories faded away, many of the elements that I found forever ingrained in my mind involved food. Tiny wild strawberries magically appeared in the field in front of our home where snow had covered it only a few weeks earlier, tangy blackberries grew on the side of the road, and the trees surrounding us were abundant with apples, cherries, and plums. We tilled and planted the garden as soon as it was dry enough to navigate, and Mom prepared her flower beds all around the house. My dad was a forager before foraging and farm-to-table became so trendy, and our life, at times, literally seemed to revolve around procuring food.

Spring brought on fiddleheads, the mineral-rich ferns that are now so coveted by high-end restaurants across America. We often trekked into the woods down by the stream on "my dad's mountain" to harvest them and bring them back in a little wicker basket. My mom cooked them with oil and vinegar, but I can't recall ever liking them at all.

Our rhubarb patch was like clockwork, rising up from the newly fertile earth each spring, which brought on my mom's pies, both with apple and the pure rhubarb itself with vanilla ice cream. She always served it warm, the crust buttery and flaky. My grandmother, Nana, would mock me while I ate my first bite:

"More pie, Mum?" she would say, in advance of my expressing those exact words. To say I had a sweet tooth would be an understatement.

I remember one year my uncles and father decided to buy their own livestock, and "Bill the Bull" was kept in a makeshift pen on my Uncle Richard's lawn before heading off to the slaughterhouse. Many seasons, my dad and his friends bought a pig and took it up to Blue Hill where a crafty local dude would magically transform it into thick slabs of smoky, fatty bacon.

We tapped the trees out in the woods behind the house, producing gallons of the clean maple sap before reducing it in the contraption my dad set up outside, the reduction of about forty times resulting in the most golden, ethereal form of sweetener. And my dad would don his white net hat and full-length coat of beekeeping armor, gloves and all, to tend the hives he installed, despite having an extremely severe allergy to bee stings.

My parents taught us the beauty of being self-sufficient, and if plants were the heart of our food supply chain, hunting and fishing were the cornerstones. One summer, we got a license to trap lobsters, and we'd often head out in our little boat in the early evening, just before dusk, to pluck our dinner from the sweet and salty ocean.

We camouflaged ourselves, going after wild duck and woodcock, and traipsed through the early autumn leaves trying to flush out partridge and pheasants. We shot the occasional rabbit, and I even received a coveted moose-hunting license one year.

While I enjoyed hunting, I never got into fishing, though I often went along anyway. We fly-fished in wading boots in the river by my dad's mountain, trolled for mackerel in the bay, and scoured every brook, stream, lake, and inlet within a hundred miles, it seemed. We even set up a hut and fire and drilled through the ice of Swan Lake in sub-zero temperatures. Still, fishing wasn't my thing, and the slimy texture of a live fish, the smell of its guts when being cleaned, even the oily aroma from cooking them . . . none of it appealed to me.

Crustaceans were a different story. Scallops, in all their nutty, buttery glory, could be wonderful—especially with golden breadcrumbs and parsley. Lobster speaks for itself. Even at a young age, I was fanatical about sourcing the freshest ingredients. I knew which crabmeat pickers picked on which days and would arrive at their shops while the meat was still warm, barely in the refrigerator.

Despite all this food-gathering experience, the last thing I wanted to deal with was the actual cooking. I had already grown to love fine dining, but there was none of that in Searsport. Our primary restaurant was a greasy spoon and soft-serve place called Jordan's, a rambling building that had been extended a few times to seat about a hundred and fifty, plus three big takeaway windows where the entire town seemed to feed themselves in the summer. This was Maine's version of *Happy Days*—all good vibes, despite the fact that most of the food was poison.

I'd mowed lawns on Savage Road and done some odd jobs around town, but until I turned fourteen, I never held a real job. My parents finally insisted I start learning how to work and support myself, so I applied at the only place in town that would hire a kid: Jordan's. Unlike in New York City or Los Angeles, small towns don't typically have a population of adults looking for dishwashing jobs, so these fall to the kids, the summer-job hopefuls. Dishwashing gives you a great insight into the backbone of a restaurant.

Although I'd loved restaurants since I was as young as can be, I never had a desire to be back there in a sweaty, steamy room full of mostly men in white *Howdy Doody* uniforms. Jordan's chefs looked miserable, back there wiping their brows from the summer heat, the salamander melting cheese for burgers, the non-stop bubbling fryolator pumping out frozen fries, and the overall oily stench in the air from overcooked seafood, powdered and boxed ice cream mix, processed everything, and sodium galore. This was Jordan's. I worked there for an entire summer and never saw a vegetable. I felt like crap, and aside from the ice cream sandwiches I picked at (because the walk-in box was right next to the dishwasher), I don't recall eating much of anything.

The chef was a wisecracker named Gary, a congenial guy with a wry sense of humor, and he was always up for a party. I was a few years under the legal drinking age, but it never stopped him from getting me into trouble. One of my busiest nights, a Saturday, left me so backed up on dishes that they were piled up on the floor—it seemed like it would be two hours before I could ever cycle these all through and go home. So, when Gary winked at me while he stuck a couple six packs of Lowenbrau just outside the kitchen door, it didn't really excite me.

"I have all these dishes to do. I can't go out tonight."

Gary looked at me like I was speaking a foreign language.

"What dishes?" he said, as he proceeded to pick up and drop a couple dozen of them on the floor, and a few into the trash, creating a mash up of broken plates all over my station. "You're done."

He helped me scoop it all into the garbage. I guess the used plates may only have cost a quarter each, so that probably didn't matter. Our manager only came in once a week and would never realize it anyway.

This seemed to be a time when I started to let go of my youth and embrace a bit of responsibility. I was heading into high school, and sports were more of a challenge. Instead of competing on teams with the same friends I'd had for the last ten years, I would soon be a freshman, three years behind the seniors who would command the key positions in sports and in the high school pecking order.

While I'd been accustomed to being the tallest in my class as a child, a few of my classmates passed me in junior high, and by the time high school rolled around, I was settling into being average height. Some of the little guys I'd pushed around when I was small were now looking down at me, and I had to adjust my approach to life and sports pretty quickly. No longer was I the center on the basketball team who could intimidate with my size or the batter hitting cleanup whose size alone would scare the pitcher into walking me. My new life required speed, dexterity, skills, and navigation. There was only one problem, and it was a big one. I'd started to put on excess weight due to my romance with sugar and the lack of nutrients in my diet. My parents pushed vegetables on me, and I, in turn, pushed them under my napkin, waiting until nobody was watching to swiftly discard them.

Life took a turn I never expected around this time, just after my fifteenth birthday. We had swimming night once a week during the winter in the next town over, Belfast. They had a large indoor pool, and since Searsport was too small for a swim team, we were able to ride a bus over and spend the evening splashing around. It's remarkable how disconnected we can become from our bodies and our internal health when we simply let go. This would be my first and last experience with that disconnection, and it was harsh.

Standing on the side of the pool, laughing and enjoying the evening like all my other friends, I was about to jump back in when one of my wiry—at times insensitive—friends, Todd, walked up to me, poked at my abdomen, and smiled derisively.

"Eww, what is this, Jell-O? What happened to you?" he asked, surveying the soft pudge of my belly.

I felt suddenly frozen, jolted out of my comfort zone. More than embarrassment, this was a pure wake-up call. I was furious—at myself. It felt like he'd dropped a bucket of ice on me, and I asked myself, *Why would I allow my diet to make me so unhealthy?* I knew better than that. One thing was for certain: this situation had to change course . . . and fast.

I immediately resolved to stop eating junk food and sugar, swore off butter entirely, and started preparing many of my own meals, which meant a lot of whole wheat pasta with tomato sauce—boring stuff, but clean and light. My mom bought snacks for me from the organic hippie co-op, like whole grain, dog-biscuit-tasting little crackers and breads and organic peanut butters, and I started to eat more fruit. I rarely ate the same food as the rest of the family, and I swore off school lunches for good. My body quickly responded. I began to lean out, and by the next summer, I was a different athlete and a different person.

My good friend Karen lived down by the town park next to a makeshift gym in her neighbor's garage. It was apparently owned by a science teacher from the next town over, and most evenings, the doors to the garage were open, revealing half a dozen grunting, sweating muscle heads.

Although there was no sign on the place and certainly no phone number, it was referred to as "Ed's Gym"—a typical two-car garage, but instead of cars and gardening equipment, it was jam-packed with weight benches, squat racks, pulleys and chains, and endless pounds of iron. Posters of Arnold and Lou, as well as the up-and-coming female bodybuilders, were on the walls, along with a few quotes here and there: "No pain, no gain!" No Tolstoy, but still, it was inspiring to see that in a small, quiet town where most young men were drinking Budweisers and grilling venison steaks.

The gym rats would do their workout and then jog around town in their short shorts, muscles bulging. They looked like aliens, but in a good way. I knew it was not enough to just eat well and participate in sports, even though conventional wisdom in the early '80s was that lifting weights would hamper flexibility and ruin your game. I didn't believe it and joined. This added a whole new layer to my understanding of my body.

I don't have the type of body that bulks up or gets ripped, so lifting weights was simply a way for me to become stronger and firmer and to learn how to isolate muscles. It did wonders for me, and soon my friend Kevin joined. We continued lifting through high school, despite the fact that our crazy basketball coach would make wisecracks throughout practice about how we weren't flexible because we were "lifting those weights." Kevin and I didn't care; we were getting strong, and we felt great. Coupled with my diet, I was a new person with more clarity, speed, self-confidence, and overall sense of balance.

These short years were pretty wonderful. Ed, from Ed's Gym, became a mentor to us, and we tried his Pritikin diet and learned to chow down on raw almonds and whole grains way before they became a fad. I'd occasionally go off and enjoy a chocolate feast or have something rich, but the times that happened were few and far between. I discovered the deep connection between mind, body, and spirit, and all through high school, things flowed well. Mind. Body. Spirit. You can't have one or two without the others.

This sense of balance led me to believe that I could have whatever I set my mind to, and I put that theory to the test. I was president of my Student Council, captain of sports teams, and had a lovely girlfriend. Life was good for me, and the key to it all was my health.

RISOTTO FRUTTI DI MARE

It's a magical way to spend a long afternoon: sipping wine, savoring the aroma of simmering onion, steamed shellfish, and nutty arborio rice while prepping this classic Italian recipe. Tiny, sweet shrimp, buttery bay scallops, and gently cooked calamari mingling with the carefully cooked and lovingly stirred grains, finished with a knob of salty butter, a handful of grassy parsley, and freshly chopped tomato. Add a touch of parmesan to seal in the richness.

OPTIMIST

Change always seemed to be good for me—though I sometimes leave situations too early before I am able to fully realize the fruits of my time there. I recognized my pattern early on. I was never the superstar who could walk into a room or a new environment and take over immediately, but I always found my groove pretty quickly. Even though I was a kid from a town of fifteen hundred people, dropped onto a huge college campus with a couple thousand new freshman, dozens of fraternities, and clubs of every kind, my natural ability to get along with others, lead, and make friends seemed to kick in.

Since my first college roommate was a friend from high school, I felt pretty comfortable in our new dorm and, by habit, started to form a little life that centered around our third-floor clique and the commons we shared with two other dorms. That first semester flew by—lots of Napoli's pizza, video games in the lobby of the dorm, a few new friends, and a beautiful blonde girl named Donna—my first post-Searsport girlfriend.

The campus was definitely intimidating, but by the time the second semester rolled around, I'd been recruited at one of the nastiest, wildest, filthiest, and most popular fraternities on the campus: Sigma Nu. I jumped at the opportunity to join when a friend from high school who was a frat brother there invited me.

This place was a real zoo—a massive, once-stately, three-story, white building right out of *Animal House*. The floors and doors creaked, and it had a permanent aroma of musk, dust, and keg beer. Put forty high-testosterone guys in a home together without an ounce of domestic skill among them and this is what you get.

The first floor had a huge sectional couch that must have hid countless germs. There was a ping pong table in a small room to the left. The dining room held a giant table that could probably seat fifty people and looked like something left over from a castle. The basement was a party room with a makeshift bar, a rusty weight bench, and some other debris, and a little kitchen where the kind cook, Gloria, tried to satiate the beasts. The top two floors consisted of bedrooms and "The Ram," a massive rectangular room with bunks where most of the brothers slept.

This house was a cast of characters, recruited with some genius behind the process: a number of athletes, a few scholars, and some cool guys. After a single semester of parties, fights, pranks, and absolutely horrendous sanitation and food, I was ready to get out and moved off campus to an apartment.

On campus, there were a few classes offered that everyone would sign up for—usually courses where the instructor was so lazy he would teach the same curriculum and administer the same test year after year. It was in one of these classes that I first met Mike. While I was sitting pretty far back, struggling to get through the midterm test, the guy next to me, a small but tough gangster-looking kid in a tight black sweater and black jeans, elbowed my left arm.

"Yo, move your arm. I can't see," he snapped in an accent that wasn't quite Boston, perhaps Brooklyn or some other tough New York neighborhood where the thugs hang out. This punk wanted to see my answers.

"I'm left-handed. This is how I write."

I had seen Mike around campus. He was one of the studs, a city-born football star who was always with the other football stars, the Masters of the Universe at this school. I shook it off and felt a little like I needed to wash my hands.

Mike and I would have another run-in a few weeks later, which began with some threats and a bit of shoving, but ended with a hug. I had an unlikely new friend, and a few weeks later, he introduced me to my first true love: New York City.

It was a Friday night, and I was in the back of a big old Delta 88, some early-'80s club music roaring out of its four speakers and two guys in leather sitting in the front seat. We made a quick stop at Burger King and hit I-95, heading to New York City. Another football player, Gary Hufnagle—or "Huff"—was driving, and Mike was riding shotgun. We were going to a party on the Upper East Side.

I'd never set foot on the ground in New York City and had only passed through once, in the backseat of my parents' Cadillac. I recall diving to the floor when my dad drove through Times Square, which, in those days, reeked of filth and danger. I had spent very little time outside of Waldo County and, other than a few trips with my parents to Pennsylvania and Florida, hadn't really left Maine. This was my only point of reference.

After arriving in the city, we spent the first night at a comedian's house, a friend of Mike's brother, and the next day, we walked through Central Park and around the East 60s. The neighborhood was bursting with life, filled with shops and delis and restaurants and elegant people on all the streets. It all felt so out of reach, but comfortable at the same time.

The party later that night reminded me of the quintessential New York I'd seen on television. This was so far away, so different from Searsport. And yet, it fascinated me.

On the ride back, our energy was deflated from too little sleep and too much drinking, so we bought some pizza and slept in the car. Monday morning found me feeling pretty hazy and out of it, but New York was in my blood. I felt as if I'd visited another planet, and I couldn't wait to get back.

Mike and Huff graduated that year, as did many of my other friends, and the rest of my years in college seemed like a blur to me. I went home each summer to work at Geddy's, a local bar, and then headed back to school each fall to pursue a major in pre-law, looking forward to the day I would move to New York City.

It was a very quiet time in my life. I got into a routine of exercise—mostly running—paying attention to my studies, and spending many quiet nights at the apartment making dinner for myself. There was a health food store across the street, and I kept it simple: mostly brown rice and grains, a little dairy, and some vegetables or chicken. Life was simple.

During my breaks, I tried to get to New York to see Mike. In the spring of my senior year, I really felt the city pulling me in. While my other friends went spring skiing or headed down to one of the beaches in Florida for Spring Break, I was excited to go to New York.

I will never forget the first time I drove alone into the city, down FDR Drive and exiting on 59th Street right into the flow of traffic. I had never driven into the city on my own, and I felt a deep connection—it was as if the thousands of cars, mostly yellow, propelled me forward. Before I knew it, I was parked around the corner from the 64th Street apartment Mike now shared with his brother.

Our routine that week was exhausting, more for Mike than for me. Mike worked all day while I explored the city—from Grand Central, into Bloomingdales, and up, down, and across Manhattan. Taking in that magic, I knew that New York had layers and layers of meaningful lessons for me, and I was smitten.

As soon as Mike got home from work, I'd share news of my day, and we'd have something to eat and a beer together. For dinner most nights, I walked from his apartment on Lex and 64th in the early evening over to a take-out place called Chicken Kitchen and bought a whole chicken for about $4.99.

On the way there, I always passed a place that that would haunt me for years. It was a gorgeous restaurant with a horseshoe-shaped bar. This was Alo Alo. Inside were the most beautiful people I'd ever seen in my life: well-dressed New Yorkers and Europeans, dressed mostly in black, drinking fancy cocktails in the dimly lit room with glowing triangular lights. Mannequins were on the wall, giving the place a sense of whimsy, but it was all done in such an elegant manner that it worked. As comfortable as I was in social settings, this place intimidated me. Mike said it was for the rich people.

After our filling-but-cheap dinner, Mike and I went out, usually until two or three in the morning, and always ended up back at the apartment watching television or laughing about whatever trouble we'd gotten into. Then Mike would lay down under a blanket on the floor, still in his suit from work. The next morning, he'd wake up, put his shoes on, wet his hair, and go back to work, and the ritual would begin all over again when he came home.

That Spring Break trip solidified my plans; by the time I graduated from college, I began making arrangements to move to New York.

I needed a job and an apartment, so I immediately started commuting into the city with applications and simultaneously tried to get a restaurant position in Connecticut, where I was staying with a friend and her family.

I wanted to tend bar, but a few places turned me down as I was either too young or too inexperienced. Then someone suggested the Five Mile River Grille, a popular place in a small sailing town called Rowayton.

The owner, Nick, was a slick, good-looking, and well-dressed man. I was healthy and tan, and he mentioned something about Tom Cruise (the movie *Top Gun* had just come out). I was hired on the spot.

I spent the summer bartending and making more money than I ever had in my life.

I had a loyal crowd, a couple drinks named after me, and free rein with the music. I blasted Mick Jagger, created a bunch of ridiculous drinks made from Malibu Rum, and had a blast.

I made a few friends, although the culture there wasn't one I was completely comfortable with. It was very preppy, filled with a lot of wealthy kids who didn't have summer jobs and drank like fish. Plenty of attractive girls came to the bar, but I just didn't connect with anyone—with the exception of the hostess, Kirsten. She was intimidating, a tall and elegant natural beauty with the body of a ballerina, who floated through the dining room.

One night, she came up to the bar and asked for a Perrier. We chatted—she had gone to school in New York, where she grew up, and did some studies abroad. She was a Francophile. I hadn't left the country, so this was another boundary for me. She was engaging, but she kept it short and left me standing there, nearly breathless.

A month later, Kirsten and I were in a serious relationship and talked of moving to New York together.

Before we started our lives in New York, Kirsten and I decided to take a detour to visit my old boss Geddy in Kauai, Hawaii. Our parents weren't too happy about this, but we had our minds set and bought one-way tickets. Just before we left, we spent one last night in New York. It was Labor

Day weekend, and the city was dead. We went for a drink at Rupert's, a dumpy pub on the West Side where Mike's brother, Pete, was the bartender. Pete hooked us up with a few drinks, and we asked him where to have dinner.

"Elio's on the Upper East Side."

Entering Elio's, my life completely changed. The room had a glow, both from lighting and the dark wood; the tables were close together, yet it still felt cozy. The menu was in Italian, and we had to ask a few questions.

"What is riz-otto?"

"Rice."

"Cap-preece?"

"Mozzarella and tomatoes. Have the Risotto Porcini," demanded the white-haired patriarch of the dining room. So we did.

A tall, disheveled, but distinguished-looking, twitchy man sat at the bar alone, holding a paper bag and sipping a glass of wine. He occasionally got up to play with the lights or change the music, which was just a touch louder than it should have been and gave the place a good vibe. He was the owner, and I zeroed in on him like a heat-seeking missile. I couldn't imagine a better life than producing your own show, which also happened to include the most mind-blowing food on the planet. I wanted to do what Elio did, to own my own restaurant in Manhattan.

PINEAPPLE IN A JEEP

When cold seasons have deprived you of fresh, aromatic fruits, and you first encounter them again, don't wait to indulge. Seek an unattended shady fruit stand, leave a few coins in the coffee tin, and select the sweetest smelling pineapple on the counter. Head off-road and park under the palms to cut it open. The juices run down your wrists and forearms as your taste buds come alive.

WANDERER

Everything smelled like honey and flowers. Evenings on the tropical, humid Hawaiian Islands were unlike anything I'd ever experienced. The flight from the East Coast had been a long one: six hours to California from New York, and several more to Hawaii. We had reserved a room at the Coco Palms, a rambling, tacky tourist trap in Kapaa, not far from the airport. Between us, we had less than $1,000, because we hadn't received much help from our parents. Needless to say, they were mildly disappointed to see their investments in french history and pre-law being channeled into a life on the beach. We really didn't have a plan and certainly knew we wouldn't be able to live on this remote island forever, but there we were.

"Twenty-four dollars for fruit and toast and juice?" Kirsten knew we couldn't stay here long, or we'd be out of money in less than a week.

The next day, we rented a jeep from a very tan mechanic near the airport.

"You've all got that Eastern glow . . . don't ya?" Although it was only a couple weeks past summer and we both had pretty respectable tans, nothing was hiding where we came from. We were haoles, through and through.

I hadn't seen Geddy in over a year. I was conflicted about letting him know we'd arrived, since I'd left him mid-summer and he was surely still angry about it. I knew that he was volatile, partially insane, and held a grudge like no other, but I was banking on the unspoken connection we had. For all his flaws, his temper tantrums, and his unpredictability, Geddy had a way of celebrating the simple things in life on a daily basis in a way that I appreciated. He also had excellent taste—nothing ostentatious or elaborate, just simple and elegant with a good hint of nature. I knew, based on his home and lifestyle in Maine, that there would be a reason he chose to live on this Hawaiian island six months each year. It had to be incredible.

We pulled into the yard of what seemed like a little plantation, a U-shaped cobbling of buildings with one blossoming small stone cottage on the left, surrounded by manicured bushes and flowers and a couple of Geddy's cars. This was his home. It was connected to a long, narrow building that was empty except for what appeared to be a couple offices. On the right, about 200 yards from Geddy's place, was an identical stone cottage, although this one was dark, abandoned, and run-down.

"M-M-M-M-MATT!"

Geddy always kept a photo of himself from years ago with Mother Theresa, in a setting that appeared to be somewhere warm and poor; his hair was shoulder-length and his skin bronzed, revealing the rough handsomeness that he had slowly destroyed with drugs and alcohol. Here in Kilauea, Geddy's hair was long again, like in that photo, and he looked healthier, though a little bit wild. He took us for a long drive around the North Shore in his Cherokee, into a little village for an ice cream, up to Hanalei, and all the way to the end of the road where the surfers congregated.

We moved into Geddy's abandoned cottage the next day—it was a little dusty, but we got a mattress and a few basics, towels, and some used dishes. There was no electricity, so we had to get everything done before dark as candles simply were not enough to light this pitch-black place. We had an outdoor shower, which was magical, and bought an old gold Datsun with so much wear and tear you could see the pavement through the floorboards. Kirsten took a job at the deli across the street, where she made avocado sandwiches and came home with her fingernails caked with the green fruit, and I began working for Geddy's wacky friend Joel.

Joel owned a lot where part of the movie *South Pacific* was filmed, and it had a forty-foot natural waterfall that was mostly hidden by the growth of banana trees. Joel needed help clearing some of the trees and doing other grunt work around the property, so he hired me on the spot. During the day, I spent about eight hours wielding my machete and crawling through the thick trees, making space wherever Joel's other hired guy, Kent, asked me to.

Kirsten and I worked long and hard, but our escape was our early evening runs, when we'd go a few miles on the road from Kilauea down to the beach, or on weekends, hiking to Waimea Canyon.

We filled ourselves with lots of sushi and gorgeous fruits: cherimoya (when we could afford it) and tons of banana, papaya, and pineapple. You could just feel the life in this fruit—sweeter, juicer, richer, and more vibrant than anything I'd eaten on the East Coast. I grew my hair out and went barefoot whenever possible. The nourishment we received from this balmy air, the living foods, going to bed with the sun, and regular exercise made us both feel better than we ever had in our lives.

One afternoon, a couple from New York came into the shop where Kirsten was working. I was there for a lunch break. We'd only been on the island a few months, but apparently we had mellowed out pretty well because the couple could barely believe we were from the East Coast.

She was glamorous and he was sophisticated, with an air of success and confidence. We told them our plan was to move to New York again someday. I had become accustomed to visualizing my future during our hikes, imagining the restaurant in New York and becoming an entrepreneur like my father, an independent man.

"How will you get charged up again?" the glamorous woman asked. "Once you're here for a while, you lose that edge you need for New York."

Perhaps the lady was right. We were not unhappy, but we weren't inspired. We were both passionate people and had always been high achievers. I couldn't see myself cutting banana trees with Kent for much longer, and I didn't want to live on $300 a week forever. The rainy season had also started, which took away much of what we loved there. A dark cottage is one thing, but when it's cold and damp and you're stuck in there all the time, it gets old fast. The sun hadn't been out for days.

Geddy had also been away and only called to ask us to do things for him. He had become irritable in our recent conversations, eventually laying into me about his old Volvo getting wet.

The rain, the boredom, and then Geddy's meltdown made our decision for us. We sold our rust bucket to Kent for $300 and bought tickets to New York City the next week.

Our friends from college were mostly settled into jobs now, earning salaries good enough to provide them nice apartments, and many of my friends, who were older, were already two or three years into their careers. Even Mike, when we reconnected, was pounding away on his career, funneling his endless charm and world-class partying abilities into building the network that would propel his career. I had played around long enough and was determined to conquer this city. Truth be told, the adjustment wasn't easy—I wasn't ready for cranky cab drivers, the pressure of being bottled up in a subway with hundreds of other grumpy commuters, or the bitter cold. Still, New York captivated me like never before as I set my sights on the potential ahead.

We quickly found a little walk-up studio just big enough for a pull-out couch that filled the entire single room and a narrow hallway kitchen that led to a tiny, no-frills bathroom.

I needed to get a job, as we'd spent all but a couple hundred dollars on moving in, and since our parents were not going to be there for us, the pressure was intense. I knew only one way to get a job fast, so I hit the street.

We lived on a block, East 67th Street, that had only three businesses. The biggest was the headquarters of Fox News, and down the street was a bar called Nickels, named for the bar, which was made out of nickels. It seemed kind of like a jazz club restaurant for depressed New Yorkers—dark and creepy. Next to that was Christie's East, which I assumed was part of the famous Christie's Auction House, the one that made national news for its record-setting sale of Van Gogh's *Irises* for nearly $80 million. This option appealed to me the most, so I entered the small gallery, resumé in hand.

"I'd like to apply for a position," I told the first person I could find, although there wasn't much activity.

The smartly dressed woman handed me a business card. "Here, go to Park Avenue and speak to this person."

I took the card, walked down to 59th and Park, and froze in front of the massive gold doors, the dove-white awning with scripted letters, the doormen in top hats and fitted blue coats with red stripes, and the red carpet that extended from the door to the sidewalk.

"I was sent here to apply for a job."

The doorman smiled and pointed to a side entrance around the corner. I waited about an hour and was escorted to a human resource person.

"We receive hundreds of applications from art students, but Mr. Lash needs assistance with some projects, and most of our interns are off now that summer and the holidays are over." Her British accent had me. I was in a new world.

I realized that I had just been handed a miracle. The money wasn't great—just above minimum wage—but it was a full-time, forty-hours-a-week position for a few weeks. During the day, I was bored out of my mind, going through catalogs, putting books in the mail, and sorting through papers and other nonsense. I wasn't even sure they needed me, and I spent many days watching the clock.

Within a month, I had been moved down to the press department, and this was much more fun. My office mates were four attractive women, a few years older than me, all lovely and respectful of me, but also pretty focused on social climbing.

My favorite part of the job was walking the floor of the parties prior to the auctions. We weren't allowed into the auction house during the auction, but the parties had the most incredible food: tiny morsels of delicious shellfish, warm and savory French pastries with cheese, and glasses of endlessly flowing champagne.

Kirsten was working on Wall Street at Dean Witter Capital and had a crazy boss who tormented her. I was bored, but proud of my job. We were stable and putting in our time, although I was impatient.

Spring arrived in New York, and the city blossomed. All in all, life was hard, but things were improving. Long gone was the casual life I'd had in Maine and the months when time stopped in Hawaii. This was the real world, and taking our foot off the gas was not an option.

MOQUECA DE PEIXE

It's the dancing balance of fiery malagueta peppers, citrus, cilantro, and thick coconut milk with cod so moist it crumbles into the saucy stew, all absorbed by the earthy farofa. This Bahian shellfish stew evokes a deep history and will simultaneously stand up to any modernist flavors head on.

APPRENTICE

You never know what's behind a door until you walk through it. I had been hovering around one particular door for two or three weeks until I finally realized what was going on. I can still feel its serpentine, polished brass handle. The exotic ironwork hosting light fixtures above the small elegant bar, and the rich orange and deep blue fabrics on the new furniture inside remain firmly embossed in my culinary memory bank.

My lunch break while I worked at the auction house went from noon to 1 p.m., and every day I would walk to Grand Central Station or to Central Park or just roam the neighboring blocks. I never went too far; I felt pretty at home in the East 60s where I lived and worked. With increasing frequency, I kept finding myself drawn, magnet-like, to the front of a new restaurant, Malvasia, being constructed at 108 East 60th Street.

The handsome young chef and owner, Gennaro, later told me that Malvasia is a variety of wine grapes that is well known in Sicily, and particularly on the Island of Lipari, where Gennaro was from. He'd been recruited to the States for a project by the famed producer Dino De Laurentis and had worked around Manhattan at a few places—most notably at Bice, a powerhouse Italian place in Midtown. A wealthy doctor had met him there and offered to back him in his own place, and so the renovation began.

After about three weeks of peering in to see the latest developments, I noticed a menu box outside. It was as if all of my favorite foods had been assigned to one kitchen, a block from my work! And it included not one, but two risotto dishes. I can recite it today, despite the fact I haven't read the menu in twenty-five years: rigatoni with eggplant, tomato and salty ricotta, pasta with sardines, wild fennel and raisins, risotto with shrimp and arugula. This menu rocked.

While I was reading over the menu, the fresh-faced young manager appeared at the door. He must have seen something in me, and I owe him gratitude for being the first of several visionaries who not only believed in me but saw potential that I could not even imagine myself.

"Do you want a job?"

I stuttered a bit and looked at him, a well-dressed, pleasant-looking guy in a nice sport coat. He seemed confident and looked like a true New Yorker.

"I'm David Pearlberg," he said as he quickly extended his arm to its full length to shake my hand. He had a jovial smile, was average height, and didn't appear to be very athletic, which I took as a sign that he was a real restaurant guy.

The next thing I knew, I was working at Malvasia, training in the dining room, and while I was fearful of being on the floor, I loved every minute of the learning. Raul, our busboy, brought warm, oily focaccia to every table, and the waiters were a real pro crew: there was Vincent, the Cuban with a twangy voice, who had a few sugar daddies while he worked his shifts; Bill, in his spectacles as thick as steel and with the posture of a penguin; and Gary, who worked in film and was always a bit slow but super-thorough.

After I'd worked at Malvasia for about a month, Gennaro stopped me as I was dropping an espresso off in his tiny office next to the mezzanine dining room.

"Why you go to college and then work in restaurant?"

His voice reminded me of my dad's a bit, a natural-born teacher and leader, but in a soft way.

"I want to open a restaurant in New York."

Gennaro didn't have to think about that one. "If you want to open a restaurant, you need to learn the kitchen. Come to the kitchen tomorrow."

I had been back there, of course, to pick up food and to take dishes back to the dishwasher. It was a madhouse. The dining room was gorgeous and impeccably designed by the famous Adam Tihany, but they must have run out of money when they reached the back because it seemed the kitchen was left over from the previous tenant, another Italian restaurant. Despite the dingy appearance, I knew that kitchen held a special kind of magic that I couldn't wait to see.

The next day, I arrived just after lunch and headed back to the kitchen. The sous chef, Luca, sent me downstairs with a grunt to get my chef coat and pants. Rafael, a prep cook, was making ravioli in a hallway down there, filling each little pouch with an exquisite-looking spinach and ricotta puree, and a blue-eyed dishwasher, Francisco, was having his staff meal on a milk crate. This underground world supported New York, and while it had not excited me in the least at Jordan's with the fast, greasy food, the soulful cuisine of Italy had my senses buzzing.

Once changed, I came back up to the kitchen, to the main stage. The key players were already there—Pierro, Gennaro, Luca, and last but not least, Guiseppe, the wrangly, wiry, nasty Sicilian on the line who looked fresh out of Rikers Island. The kitchen was fairly segregated: all Italian on the line, all Mexican on prep and dishwashing, and one American, Beth, running pastry. Gennaro brought me to the butcher block and quietly, carefully, showed me how to filet a beautiful salmon, and then sent me to work with Luca on the broiler/grill station.

Mammoth veal chops were marinating in rosemary and would be grilled with wild mushrooms; swordfish was drenched in olive oil, charred, and served with potatoes, olives, sun-dried tomatoes, and more rosemary; vegetables were grilled with tons of herbs and warm goat cheese. This food was simple and wonderful. Aside from Guiseppe intentionally splattering my wrists with hot oil on occasion—my rite of passage—I was having the best time of my life. I loved the clean, crisp flavors and the intensity of the kitchen.

I also spent some time working in pastry with Beth, a graduate of a relatively new culinary school, the French Culinary Institute. Beth was a wise and shrewd New Yorker, pumping out delicious versions of Gennaro's favorite sweets: cassata siciliana, tiramisu, biscotti, gelato, and lemon tart. I loved Beth's station; although I wasn't as much of a junk foodie as I had been in my youth, I was still a fan of sweets at that point in my life. I worked with Beth a couple days a week, and she convinced me that, despite everything I was learning at Malvasia, I still needed some structured training. She thought the team of Italians that I so revered were all barbarians, and I saw her point, so I found my way into the French Culinary Institute's six-month program, Classical French Techniques.

My life had taken quite a turn, and I loved it. I woke up at 5:30 every morning and made my way down to Broadway and Grand to take eight hours of classes, then headed straight to Malvasia to work six nights a week.

Culinary school was everything I imagined it would be: a structured environment where you enter with no skills, are handed a rollup with a knife kit, put on a uniform that won't fit by the time you graduate (all the salt and butter), and go through the motions, learning dishes from French restaurants in the 1800s.

I'd love to be kind, but the reality is my instructors, save one, were chefs who'd been through the ringer in the industry and couldn't hack the hours on the line anymore. None of them had been through the French Culinary's programs. My chef, Mike, was a lovely, sweet man, and Bob the Butcher taught us about tough love, but we really only learned technique—it wasn't about ingredients. The walk-in was usually populated by a few old potatoes and tomatoes, fish was always flounder, and herbs aside from chervil were scarce. The attention to technique was wonderful, but I never saw a dish in the entire six months that I wanted to emulate. Still, I knew that this overly seasoned, butter-heavy stuff was what was generating buzz and stars in the NYC restaurant scene.

It was with a heavy heart that I followed one of my classmates to La Caravelle, one of the city's most well-regarded French restaurants. What a history this place had! It was owned by an heir to the Hotel Bristol in Paris. The chef was a tough ex-boxer named David Ruggierio, and he stocked the kitchen with a team that made the Italians at Malvasia look like carnival misfits. Gennaro was kind enough to let me continue helping out at Malvasia, but we both realized I needed to grow my career.

Three weeks into La Caravelle, I was hating every minute of it. Instead of the fresh citrus, wild herbs, and pristine seafood, we were serving escargot from a can over a ring mold of cous cous, surrounded by a 3,000-calorie sauce of red wine reduced, and mounted with pounds of butter. Every dish was like this. The basement kitchen was hot, the team fought over mise en place, and the food made me ill to think about.

I went crawling back to Gennaro, asking to return to Malvasia.

"French food is all butter. I miss it here."

"But you need to have this education. Stay with it," he advised.

I did that for as long as I could, miserable every minute of it, and one day I got a call from David, the manager who'd hired me at Malvasia.

"I've been hired as the General Manager of Alo Alo and would like you to be the Executive Chef."

My heart was pumping. I knew I'd take it. Alo Alo was the very same restaurant I'd walked by so many times on the way to Chicken Kitchen when I was visiting Mike back in college, and like Malvasia, it had been designed by Adam Tihany. Everyone knew it as a once super-hot place in a great location, but it had lost popularity due to a reputation for its terrible food.

David said he took the job on one condition: that he could bring in a new chef. He offered me $60,000, which was about three times what I'd ever made in my life. I gave this offer a huge bear hug, put in my notice at La Caravelle, and went to discuss it with Gennaro.

"I don't think you are ready for this. If I were you, I would not go to Alo Alo," Gennaro told me in a very calculated voice.

In fact, pretty much everyone told me I wasn't ready, but I was determined not to pass up the opportunity.

My first day, I walked in to meet the staff. The owners had decided not to fire anyone, but rather to have me come in and manage the staff that was there. Before I ever set foot in the place, I poured my heart into a menu that respected the modern Italian concept and added a touch of elegance from my recent French training. There was only one problem: the kitchen was full of lazy, stagnant chefs who thought the miserable food they were selling was good.

It was a disaster. The kitchen was filthy, unorganized, and nearly everything was pre-plated. Even though it takes thirty seconds to plate a caprese—the classic tomato-mozzarella-basil appetizer—they had them stacked up in the fridge for days and removed the plastic before sending it into the million-dollar dining room. My first day was brutal: I opened that fridge and tossed everything in the garbage—not for effect, but because that is where it belonged. This was a restaurant designed by one of the best restaurant designers in NYC, with a $25,000-a-month rent, and owned by a famous Brazilian nightlife impresario. Just a few years earlier, Alo Alo had received two stars in the *New York Times*, and now it was serving absolutely disgusting food. One infamous dish on the menu was Pasta con Tonno, translated here as overcooked noodles with butter and canned tuna. It was a vile dish.

Within a month, I'd replaced 80 percent of the kitchen staff and most of the suppliers, been attacked by the butcher (he slipped in water trying to take a swing at me, and I elbowed him onto the floor), and even made Abran, the sweetest cook ever, cry. I wasn't going to squander this opportunity so a few lazy cooks could make their lives easier.

The regulars were a bit outraged when I removed their crappy comfort pseudo-Italian food from the menu and replaced it with dishes inspired by my work at Malvasia, my new love for Mediterranean cuisine, and my French training. I was worried; sales were totally flat, and it seemed I'd joined a graveyard. Then, we had not one, but three visits from the infamous Insatiable Critic, Gael Green from *New York Magazine*. In an instant, things changed.

The caption was simple: "Alo Again."

The review was short, but complimentary and just vague enough to pique curiosity:

> Alo twice is looking good with Matthew Kenney, by way of Malvasia and La Caravelle, behind the griddle and David Pearlberg running the show for Brazilian Impresario Ricardo Amaral.[1]

We were packed the next day and for several months after. This review was followed by several more in other NYC publications, and my career slowly kicked into gear. The press was nice, but what I really I loved was heading into that kitchen every day and putting out food I was passionate about. The beauty of the hospitality industry is that you are on stage night after night, and you have a deep connection to the product, coming and going.

While all this was going on, life stabilized. Kirsten and I had a few extra dollars, which we used to develop a comfortable but simple lifestyle. We dined out as much as we could, often showing up at the city's most revered restaurant, Bouley, at close to midnight for a four-star meal. I loved going out, and between new movies, the city's culture, and great restaurants, I felt like my life was a constant rotation of stimulation. She and I also met for lunch often, usually in the neighborhood.

Buoyed by our improved life and compatibility, we found ourselves discussing marriage over lunch one day across from Alo Alo at a Southwestern restaurant called Arizona 206, a *New York Times* three-star place with brilliant, vibrant food by chef Marilyn Frobuccino.

I somehow blurted it out, and Kirsten clarified the question for me. "You want to marry me?"

And so we did. Before I could blink, we had a wedding date and honeymoon plans. Around the same time, I was invited by the owners of Alo Alo to be the chef of the new Brazilian restaurant they were planning in Gramercy Park: Banana Café. It was a sister to Ricardo's place in Rio, a tongue-in-cheek, trendy bi-level place that jammed day and night. The owners wanted me to spend some time in Brazil to get a feel for what they had in mind for the new restaurant, but the restaurant was set to open in just a few months, so I arranged a quick honeymoon for Kirsten and me in San Francisco and Napa and then planned to head straight to Brazil as soon as we returned home.

San Francisco's food scene was ideal for me, with fresher ingredients than I'd seen on the East Coast and a purity to the food that I embraced. We visited some of the early pioneer restaurants of those days: Bruce Cost's Monsoon, where we had the tea-smoked duck three days in a row; Zuni Café for chicken; Joyce Goldstein's Square One; the quirky and delicious little China Moon; and, of course, the iconic Stars, founded by Jeremiah Tower.

I was back in New York just long enough to catch a breath, check on Alo Alo, and do some laundry before I was on the plane to Rio. This was my first food trip for work, and I was excited, having no idea what to expect.

Ricardo put me up at a hotel by the beach, and I walked back and forth to the restaurant, where I learned some Brazilian classics: pao de queijo (known to Americans as cheese bread); moqueca de peixe; dende, the Bahian fish stew loaded with flavor from coconut, tomato, cilantro, and palm oil; and fiery malagueta peppers. This experience was meant to inspire my menu for Banana Café, not direct it, so I took a lot of cues from the citrus, tropical fruits, heat, and cilantro, and, of course, we had to have bananas.

We ran into a few hurdles obtaining a liquor license, but after a public fight, we were nearly ready. The restaurant in New York was different than the successful business model in Brazil. First off, Banana Café was much bigger: a three-level beast meant to have a club/lounge in the basement, a big bar, two floors of dining, and an open kitchen. The designer was a brash, loud, cigar-chomping old Frenchman named Serge Sassouni, apparently someone who had done some great nightclubs in Paris. He seemed like a charlatan to me; he went to every discount shop in America to find parodies of Brazil. While the Rio location was tacky but done in nice materials and all came together as a cool tropical bistro, New York was a sticky, cheap comedy of design. Ricardo was brilliant, but he had no involvement in the operation, the design, or anything. As a result, the place was hideous and had nothing to do with the original. Nobody seemed to notice, though, as we did 350 covers on opening night and were routinely booked until 1 a.m. Stretch limos lined 22nd Street every evening, and it didn't hurt that John Casablanca's Elite Modeling Agency was upstairs.

We had a fun little menu that earned us a star in the *New York Times*. Brazilian crab salad with hearts of palm and avocado, spicy little pizzas with duck and wild mushroom, those Brazilian classics I'd made in Rio, and some protein-heavy staples: veal chop, grilled salmon, and lamb shank. This was heavy food, and yet, the place was filled with models and celebrities. Shortly after opening, Donald Trump showed up and walked the floor with O. J. Simpson, shaking a few hands and leaving. Most of the early nights were like this: models, celebrities, and New Yorkers trying to be trendy.

We had a few hiccups, like the night we booked four hundred reservations at the same time. Someone had the brilliant idea to seat all three levels at once on New Year's Eve so that everyone could celebrate together. At 3 a.m., order tickets were in a pile on the floor, and we were still getting entrees out. This fiasco was the base of a nightmare I had over and over for at least ten years afterward.

Still, Ricardo taught us to take it all in stride. One night, with a packed dining room and music cranking loud, the huge back bar, carrying hundreds of glasses, bottles, and candles, gave way to the weight of its considerable inventory and came crashing down in a thunderous roar that hushed the entire place. It really took the edge off the buzz in the room, as everyone waited to see how it would affect the festivities.

Ricardo happened to be in the middle of the first floor that night with a group of socialites. Standing up with his head toward the sky, his little barrel chest puffed out, and his short arms wide, he made a few loud claps, cried, “OOOOOPAAAAA!” and toasted his glass to the room. The party went on.

Despite the wackiness of the place, Bryan Miller, the *New York Times* food critic, gave us a decent—though not completely accurate—review. His opening pretty much summed up my first major review: “A Brazilian theme, a lot of noise, and even some Brazilian food.”

He went on:

> It’s like awakening from a dream and finding yourself in a hip Manhattan restaurant, circa 1985. First, there is the aggressively perfumed, out-of-season-tanned crowd at the reservation desk. Thudding pop music renders communication with the hostess about as easy as talking on a pay phone from a busy subway platform. Curiously, your name doesn’t seem to be in the reservation book, but, you are assured, by the time you check your coats ($2 minimum), the problem should be solved.
>
> Is Banana Café a brilliant stroke of kitsch for the ’90s or a fatuous throwback? Three clamorous visits reveal that it is a bit of both, anchored by an able kitchen that helps keep the 250 seats filled.[2]

While I'd expected more than one star, it was actually a gift for a place like that. So, we stayed busy. Despite the apparent success, the Banana Café wasn't my scene; it did not fulfill my creative or culinary ambitions, and after a year, I began exploring my options. I'd become friends with the young chef Bobby Flay of Mesa Grill around the corner and was jealous that he had a place that was truly about food. Banana Café was definitely showing subtle signs of slowing down, and the writing seemed to be on the wall one weekday when the city was buzzing and Ricardo visited. It was an oddly quiet night; we had only eighty reservations. The mezzanine was closed, and there were no parties downstairs. He sat in the upstairs office with a somber look on his face.

"Banana Café feels sad."

Even though the weekends were still booked up, he knew, and I knew he knew, that Banana Café was heading into the ditch. It was just a matter of time.

NORTH AFRICAN INSPIRED CHICKEN

When traveling, taste as much as possible, exercise your palate, open your senses—and if you're a chef, bring that experience back to the kitchen. This is the way an ordinary chicken finds itself glowing with a gingery, saffron, honey sheen and enriched with nuggets of salty preserved lemon, picholine olives, and toasted pine nuts. Let the parsley rain over it, the heat of the ingredients releasing the freshness of the herbs.

CHEF

It was closing in on 11 p.m. one Friday at the end of a grueling dinner service. It had been unusually busy for this slowly dying restaurant—we had at least four hundred guests—and it was at the point in the evening when I'd let my guard down. I'd probably had a drink or two, and was already thinking about being home with my wife and cats, but that didn't stop the calls. This one was from our manager at Alo Alo, who rarely reached out to me these days.

"A taxi cab drove through the window."

"What happened? Is everyone okay?"

"I think so. We were full, but the bar, where the car hit, was quiet, so everyone is okay. We had to comp the guests and close."

I was still a virgin to the many complications that arise in the high-intensity world of operating a business in Manhattan, but I'd lived there long enough that I'd learned to roll with the city's punches.

I jumped in a taxi myself and was there in less than twenty minutes. The lights were up, revealing the dining room in a less-than-flattering way. I could feel Alo Alo's wear and tear, the lack of energy; I acknowledged internally that this might be a sign to us all. Coincidentally, the owners were both in town from Rio de Janeiro and arrived just after I did. I must admit, for a brief moment, I suspected that cashing in an insurance policy was a motive behind this wild driver ramming his taxi into the corner of Trump Plaza at full speed, but it was just a flash. I'd seen too many TV shows. Ricardo was all class.

After some milling around and discussion about calling someone to board up the glass, we also noticed the curved frame of the building was damaged—this wasn't going to be so easy to fix. A curved glass corner covered in plywood wasn't something that would bring in the guests, and we all knew the restaurant was already bleeding. As luck would have it, our landlord was the hard-nosed Donald Trump, so we knew we were looking at some downtime, maybe weeks or possibly a couple months. I'd been considering an idea for quite some time, so in light of this disaster, I just let it out.

"Maybe it's a good opportunity to change the concept?"

Judging by the way they looked at me, I'd said the perfect thing.

"What is your idea, Matchu?" Ricardo asked in his thick accent.

"I'll work on it this weekend and show you Monday."

My little word processor was one step up from a typewriter, as this was still a year before email would launch us into a new world. Still, Mrs. Tupper's firm typing lessons from high school allowed me to crank out the two-page proposal in a couple hours. My blood was pumping at the opportunity to open a real restaurant, one with *my* food and no papier-mâché-monster mannequins or fake banana leaves hanging from columns. I was ready for Monday morning.

My proposal simply described what I was passionate about: creative, clean, Mediterranean cuisine prepared with the French technique I had learned to respect. I was mesmerized by spices from North Africa, as well as the olive oil, citrus, and fresh beautiful produce I'd grown accustomed to at Malvasia, and I wanted to incorporate those elements into this reimagined restaurant. I wanted a dining room that was open and airy and clean. I knew, at the end of the day, Ricardo respected my ability to cook, and he was ready for a change at Alo Alo. I just worried he would find the new concept too esoteric.

We met at the space late Monday morning, and I pulled out my two pages of typed notes.

"What is your idea, Matchu?" boomed Ricardo, leaning back to take a full inhale of his fat Cuban cigar.

I explained the concept in detail, especially why we needed to move away from the Northern Italian theme that was now on every corner of the Upper East Side. I spoke with enthusiasm about the cuisine we would serve. The neighborhood would love it, I explained.

"What is the name, Matchu?" he asked, failing to notice the words *Camel Bar* on my paper.

"I was thinking Camel Bar," I said. I thought casual and exotic would be a great direction.

I nearly lost their attention, but Ricardo snapped back.

"Bom, let us discuss this, and we'll call you when we get back to Brazil." Seventy-two hours later, we had a deal. They insisted I put my name on the restaurant, more in line with how most chef-owned restaurants were labeled. They agreed to fund the renovation, which we estimated to be about $250,000. I would be granted 25 percent of the business and would be responsible for overseeing the entire concept development for Matthew's. I dove into this new project headfirst, and my list-making habit served me well.

Ricardo hooked me up with a famous and eccentric Brazilian interior designer named Sig Bergamin, and thus began a wonderful creative relationship I've never been able to top. Sig was colorful and flamboyant, yet he carried the most exquisite taste. I told him I wanted the place to embody the spirit of Morocco in a subtle way, and I explained the food philosophy. He got it immediately.

We scoured the fabric showrooms and had some gorgeous old sepia slides developed to become artwork on the wall. The semicircular, pounded-copper bar surrounded two rolling library ladders leading to the wine storage. The sixteen-foot walls were covered at the base with white-washed wainscoting and capped with aged-bronze molding. Venetian tan and gray plaster covered the walls. Seven enormous white fabric-covered fans spun slowly, just missing the twelve-foot palms we strategically placed in the room. Alo Alo's open-window format gave way to tall white shutters, evoking a French Colonial spirit which was further enhanced by a long teak table at the door.

Everything about the place was sexy: the white linen chair covers, the rosemary branches in linen napkins, and the slotted, copper candle holders on the tables. The floor was beautifully laid: wide pine barn boards stained a deep rich chocolate. As Ruth Reichl, the *New York Times* food critic would note, Matthew's was "a coffee table book come to life."[3] I was in love.

Restaurants are typically put together and opened by teams, often large. These days, as many as a dozen people are involved in the building of a restaurant—some focused on branding and design, others focused on budgets, menus, packaging, service, human resources, and items like flatware. At Matthew's, I had some wonderful support, but for the most part, I was left on my own, which I was thrilled about. I worked on a $250 logo with an artist in the West Village and was on site pestering the moody, fastidious contractor on a daily basis. Choosing paper for the menus, selecting the china and silver, tasting endless bottles of wine, sourcing products, and writing menus—I poured more passion into this project than anything I'd ever done in my life.

I knew from my experience on the Upper East Side that the staff could make or break you, so I hand-selected an incredible team. The kitchen brigade consisted of many of the stars from Banana Café: Matt Scully, my right hand, was a naturally gifted leader. Jean Bailly, the French-Haitian wunderkind, infused our kitchen with an energy that nobody else could bring. Ann Yu, twenty years old and barely one hundred pounds, arms scarred with nearly enough kitchen burns to obscure what a natural beauty she was, never let up on the line. And, of course, we had "Tommy," the brilliant Thai cook who loaded us with wisdom and Thai soup for the family meal.

Our floor staff was just as talented. The all-male waiters were confident, experienced, tall, and attractive, which I knew would be helpful in cultivating LLLs (the "loyal ladies who lunch"). Our hostesses were outgoing, personable, and gorgeous, and the bartenders were old pros. I felt it was the perfect balance. We were a family, and boy, was it fun.

Menus were easy to write in those days. You just needed five seafood dishes and five beef, poultry, or game dishes—that was it. Every dish on our menu was highly original, and I was proud of the restrained exoticism of the wording: cardamom-crusted salmon; crispy duck with almonds, dates, and olives; ahi tuna tartare with fennel and green olive tapenade; Moroccan-spiced crab cakes with cumin. This was a mature menu. We used solid ingredients, and the cooking was clean. I can't imagine how I was able to tame my creativity back then, given the fact that I was only 29 and had no formal supervision or limitations. It was like handing a teenager the keys to a Ferrari and seeing him drive only sixty miles per hour.

The dining room was almost too beautiful to touch. My manager, Kim, built a flower arrangement on the expansive oak desk that took the wind out of everyone who walked through the door, and every detail was curated.

The night prior to opening, we were all there until 1 a.m., sitting at table twenty-one with Sig, devouring red wine and hypothesizing about what would make this restaurant work. It was clearly a project of passion. I learned early on that there are three types of restaurants: those you fall in love with, those you execute well but keep a professional distance from, and those that are nothing but seats and numbers. It's sad to admit it, but many people open restaurants with one thing in mind: numbers. You will never hear the word hospitality unless it comes from their expensive life coach. But I worked from a point of passion from day one.

The first Monday night was quiet, perhaps twenty covers and mostly friends. The food looked gorgeous, but lights were too bright, lights were too dark, music wasn't quite right. I was agitated and committed to being our best. Our young GM, Dennis, did his best, but he was exasperated the entire time. Before it got too late, I had enough sense to walk twelve blocks home to 72nd Street and get myself ready for day two.

Tuesday was, oddly, even quieter than day one. We had a few people trickle in, but none of the Alo Alo regulars showed up. Many had expressed their concern that we no longer served pasta, and others missed their favorite dishes. They seemed to have taken the change personally.

Day three was the same . . . for about ten minutes. At 6 p.m., the room exploded. We were packed in the dining room and two-deep at the bar, and it stayed that way all night. People were loving it! With restaurant industry folk popping in late for drinks and locals hanging out to talk to me, we became the most buzzed-about place in the area overnight. That's the thing about New York—you can labor away for months or years or even a lifetime and slowly make some waves, or perhaps make none, or you can hit it out of the park and become an overnight sensation. There is nothing like it when it happens.

That first week was one long stretch of magic. Our little kitchen staff was invigorated: blending almond oil, searing everything to order, reducing sauces on the fly, never preparing anything in advance, and loving every minute of it. The food wasn't perfect, but it was alive and shining.

When you take a physical space like that, make some adjustments to the design, write a new menu, hire a staff who loves what they do, and everything changes, it makes you think: Is life that simple? Can we simply put some passion into the equation and it will all work? Sometimes that's all it takes. Matthew's was hard work, and yet, with my competent team and our shared mission, it felt effortless at times, like conducting a symphony that had been playing together for years and loved what they did.

We live for the days in our lives when we are so excited about what we do that we bound out of bed each day, regardless of how tired we are. It can happen in a new relationship, with the birth of a child, or perhaps on a great vacation. My time at Matthew's was, for me, one of the most energetic times of my life, a period of pure intensity. I had the opportunity to share the food I loved. I served it in a setting that valued an aesthetic that people could be inspired by, and I worked with a team that felt like family; this was it for me. All the pieces were aligned, and it was magical.

MOROCCAN SPICED CARROTS

Unlock the power of crisp, fresh carrots with a well-stocked pantry of spices and aromatics. Heat a skillet until it's nearly smoking, and brown sliced wedges of the root before tossing them, still hot, with a thick dressing of cumin, cayenne, ginger, honey, and lemon. When this begins to cool, fresh cilantro, oil cured olives, and salted green pistachios bring the dish to where it belongs, in a big decorative bowl at room temperature.

S T A R

In no time at all, it seemed, the rest of the world showed up. All the critics were there—from the newly appointed Ruth Reichl at *The New York Times* to those from *Gourmet* and *Food & Wine*—and all the local New York papers raved about Matthew's. Gael Greene from *New York Magazine* included Matthew's in every "Best of" column permanently. The reviews were all solid, not a single unfavorable note. This success was in large part due to the restrained menu, which was innovative without being weird. Our service was solid, the room was stunning and alive with flowers, and visitors were given a lot of love by our family; people felt good at Matthew's.

In those early days, the crowd was a powerful mix of Europeans who congregated on the Upper East Side, ladies who lunch, the locals within a twenty-block radius who could be counted on to dine with us two or three nights each week, the foodies who follow the newspapers' recommendations, and a respectable spattering of New York and international celebrities.

Nick Ashford and Valerie Simpson, the talented duo behind the hit song "Solid as a Rock," were in weekly, drinking champagne and basking in the glory of success. Al Roker was always there with his new wife, and we had occasional visits from Jerry Seinfeld, Eric Clapton, Brooke Shields, Pat Riley from the New York Knicks, and even the Queen of Spain.

This was my living room, in a sense—except it was filled day and night with the most diverse, talented, and beautiful crowd on the planet, all without pretense. There was the diminutive talent attorney who became a close friend, Al Rosenstein, and the grumpy Dr. Levine, who complained about everything. Joan Rivers asked for ketchup with her asparagus—I can't recall what else Wonder Woman ordered, but it was a treat to have her in. Even The Donald himself, Mr. Trump, came in with his then-wife Marla, bodyguard in tow at the door.

Despite all the celebrity visits, my fondest memories are of the locals—even those who were a pain in the neck. We had "Pockets," the goofy man with glasses thicker than a coke bottle, his multiple pockets stuffed to the gills with papers, rags, and other nonsense. Then we had Gloria, the sweetest, miniature old lady who carried optimism and smiles in a fifty-gallon drum. She lit up my day when she walked in! And we had the pontificating Mr. and Mrs. Kendall, who brought their own sour wine for us to decant, since ours "wasn't good enough."

We cooked day in and day out, obsessing over the plating of every dish and never letting go of our attention to detail. As the volume grew, so did the skill of my team. By a curious twist of fate, after about six months, we had five different Matthews working at Matthew's—three in the kitchen and two in the dining room—and all were highly skilled.

I was still working eighty to one hundred hours a week, earning just enough to pay rent on my studio apartment, and I'd never signed a formal partnership agreement with the Brazilians, but it didn't matter. My star was rising. I had momentum, so I didn't want to get hung up on details.

After two solid years, the so-called "celebrity chef" life kicked in. *Food & Wine* named me one of the 10 Best New Chefs in America, and I was nominated for everything under the sun: PBS Best Chefs, Outstanding Graduate by the French Culinary Institute, Rising Star Chef nominee by The James Beard Foundation. I signed a deal to write my first book, *Mediterranean Cooking*, which was published by the noted Chronicle Books. At the time, I was sharing a summer home in the Hamptons with another young gun, Bobby Flay. Those days were a blur: work all day, run the restaurant like you mean it, get together with friends for drinks until the wee hours of the night, and start all over again.

These were also the early days of chef perks. We were invited on free trips to Morocco, Mexico, and all over the country for festivals and events, all expenses included. We began to feel entitled, although we all worked too hard to become totally spoiled. I met a number of friends and mentors on these trips, from the brilliant Paula Wolfert—my Mediterranean inspiration—to wild-child chef Todd English, who would become my partner in crime, staying out the latest, drinking the most.

The temptations were plenty, but I was never part of the "culinary underbelly," the world of hard-partying chefs who cooked in the evening and lived in their own dark world of drink and drugs. We were addicted to our careers, which were moving so fast, and oddly enough, most of us were married. Mario Batali, Bobby Flay, Tom Valenti, Todd English—though all in our late 20s and early 30s, we were married and kept in check, at least somewhat, by work and our wives.

Meanwhile, at Matthew's, cracks were starting to appear. We were completely packed every night, but expenses were very high, and Trump hadn't been paid in four months, so we owed over $100,000 in rent, and bills were piling up. My Brazilian partners had begun grumbling, saying they'd close it or sell if it didn't start making more money. This was my baby, everything I'd dreamed about, and it was a huge success on a commercial level, but the reincarnation of Banana Café hadn't really panned out, so I was just an annoyance to them at that point, and their love affair with New York was mostly over.

I had met a nasty and brilliant attorney in the Hamptons while catering a dinner with Bobby Flay. He took a liking to me, as he was a big foodie and I had donated my time for his party, and he listened as I told him about my dilemma with the Brazilians, the mounting debt with Trump, and my career in peril at the young age of thirty. He introduced me at the party to his fifty guests, along with Bobby Flay.

"This is Matthew Kenney. He is here helping Bobby, and I'm going to help him kick Trump's ass."

He proceeded to take me on the wildest roller coaster ride I can remember, guiding me through my negotiations to buy out the Brazilians, renegotiate with Trump, and own the restaurant 100 percent, alone. This journey had more drama than a three-hour Hollywood film. I flew to Brazil, and although I had not saved a dime, I offered the Brazilians $600,000 to buy Matthew's. I'd pay their $100,000 rent arrears as a deposit, assume their debt, and then make installments. This sounded easy enough, but stepping into Trump's office with no collateral, no credit, and no cash, and asking for four years to pay the $100,000 he was owed was not an easy feat. Luckily, they gave it to me and agreed that if I paid the rent, it would be credited as the deposit.

With a $100,000 deposit in place, I renegotiated the debt, vendor by vendor. I walked into that restaurant after signing my new lease with Trump and took a deep breath. I was wearing a crisp white shirt, feeling strong and a bit nervous, and sat down for an afternoon cigarette before getting to work. I recall picking up a penny on the floor, a symbol for how I was going to run this place. Six months later, I had $200,000 in the bank from operating frugally and paying attention. Life wasn't so difficult.

Things were moving fast—from culinary graduate to celebrity chef, being escorted all over the world and invited to the best parties, restaurant openings, and movie screenings. Companies would send us kitchen equipment and ingredients and endless bottles of wine.

The offers started to come in, and I wasn't planning to resist. The first was from David Sneddon, the owner of a very successful gourmet food brand on the Upper West Side. He was dining at Matthew's with one of my regulars, and, in a way I'd become accustomed to, he laid the opportunity right on the table.

"I have a good location in Midtown. Let's do something there, and if it works out, we have other locations."

That project became Mezze, my fantasy take-out food: flatbread wraps served with about sixteen Mediterranean appetizers. Sig also designed Mezze, and with its two-story, long, narrow space, it felt like a Greek food hall, all white and blue and mosaic tiles. The food was bright and clean, very light and fresh, and mostly vegetarian. The first day was packed, with a line out the door—we must have fed four hundred people.

"This place will make you rich. It's a home run," said one of our other partners.

No sooner had we opened, though, than the debt collectors started threatening us. The place we'd taken over had debt out the wazoo and was essentially insolvent. David, rather than let me get hung by his partners (he was an investor and likely had no idea how bad the situation was, other than that it was struggling), invested some more capital to buy them out, and he and I took it on our own. Mezze drew a great crowd, especially since Conde Nast and all of its glossy magazines were right around the corner. For a take-out shop, we received a ton of publicity, including all the regular suspects, the *New York Times*, *New York Magazine*, and more.

Although Mezze was fun and packed, I missed Matthew's, which had come to feel like home. I told myself that not being able to stay in one kitchen was part of growing a business, that one can't be emotional about a company, but that was the wrong answer.

With Mezze going strong, I appeared to have the Midas touch and "deal talk" grew even more pronounced. Next up was a crazy "Doctor," Selim Jacobs, who ran a junky little bistro half a block away from Matthew's. It was called Ovo and had been there since my Alo Alo days. It was decent-enough looking to fool a few of the moviegoers or Bloomingdales shoppers walking by, but I would never eat there. They were dead these days, despite having a great location. Selim offered to give me the place to take over and to be his partner. Despite the drama I had at Matthew's and Mezze with partners, I dove into it again. Although my agreement was bare bones—Al, my attorney, had basically written it on a napkin—it did state that I owned the name, Bar Anise, and that I would be paid a percentage of the revenue.

By now, I had my culinary style set and brought in Sig, who created a gorgeous room, more blue and white, antiqued mirrors and lots of tile, and touches of the Eastern Mediterranean with long, cushy benches. This would be a bar version of Mezze: small plates of vibrant and flavorful food in a rocking atmosphere with lower prices. The place was shaking the sidewalk and had a line out of the door on the first day. Reviews were tepid, especially from some of my loyal food writers who missed the adult setting of Matthew's. Still, I shrugged them off, thinking they didn't understand what we were going for.

It wasn't easy going from running a single kitchen to three, so I set up a little office in the second floor of a townhouse across from Matthew's and hired one of our hostesses, a smart and attractive French girl named Sandrine, as my personal assistant. We shared my little word processor and desk, and I hired a Russian bookkeeper to balance the financials under the oversight of a CPA. I started spending part of my time in the office, but even more time running around, looking at deals. They kept coming.

Next, I was introduced to a debonair jetsetter named Andre Balazs, a famous hotelier who owned The Chateau Marmont in LA and was building a hot new Soho place called The Mercer. Andre and I talked about projects, but after several months of talking, I wasn't sure it would happen, so I began looking around for other options in Soho.

Then, a quick hit came up—Andre's real estate people bought a hotel I knew well, the Stanhope on Fifth Avenue, across from the Metropolitan Museum, New York's center of culture. The restaurant had always been a disaster, despite having the best sidewalk café in the city. They wanted to breathe new life into the restaurant and offered it to Andre. He decided to put a hot team together, including me. We would be equal partners in building Nica's.

It was a disaster.

The place was packed with all the beautiful people you could expect to follow this crew, but the food was spotty and the service was worse. I hadn't figured out how to manage three kitchens yet, much less four at the same time, and at this location, I brought in a chef who just wasn't able to handle this type of volume. The food was clubby, upscale hotel food, and once I left my passion zone, I was lost.

While this was going on, I came to the deal table for a place in Soho. I negotiated terms to buy the cavernous space from a lady who ran a tea salon there, but before we could close, a new face entered the negotiation. He looked a bit like Ryan O'Neal, with sandy hair, a deep tan that you get from driving a Porsche convertible, and just the right amount of wrinkle in his clothing to take the edge off. He had sunglasses on because the room was bright in the late afternoon glare . . . and because he was from California.

I had started wearing reading glasses on occasion and had them on this day in anticipation of all the paperwork we'd have to rifle through.

"You look cute in glasses," California Man said. Those were his first words to me.

He explained that he was the actual owner and controlled the lease. He didn't want to sell us the lease, and that was that. He fell asleep in the conference room shortly after. Needless to say, that deal never got signed. Not to be deterred, I managed to get in touch with Boyd, California Man.

I had a trip planned to Maine that weekend with my wife and received a call from him just as I arrived at the hotel. It was one of those promising summer evenings, just before cocktail hour, when good news is amplified by the timing. He said he had visited my other restaurants and liked them.

"Let's do this project together, just us," I said.

I liked his style and thus began a business romance that lasted years. We opened Monzu, a French-Sicilian restaurant, in that space a few months later. It was inspired by my French training and love for Sicilian cuisine. Monzu was an enormous investment, and we devoted ourselves to every detail of the project.

Monzu opened strong, with a lot of buzz and very good press, including another two-star review from Ruth Reichl. The place never felt quite right, though; it was cavernous and too uptown for a downtown space. We did $2 million in revenue and still lost money the first year. It was a dilemma; everyone loved the food, but it wasn't a scene. I was in the big leagues now. To carry two hundred seats and close to $40,000 a month in rent in Soho, you needed more than good food and service.

Still, reviews were good, and in perhaps in my biggest move to date, I signed a deal to open a ten-thousand-square-foot restaurant on the East Balcony of Grand Central Station. Grand Central was about to be given a hundred-million-dollar renovation and part of it included bringing some of the top brands in the city to the terminal. One space was being taken by the Michael Jordan Steakhouse and the Cipriani team took another. I took the largest and most regal of them all, the imposing East Balcony, which had never even had a staircase before. Creating this new restaurant, Metrazur, was tremendous news and catapulted my name into a new arena.

Here I was, sitting on a budding restaurant empire—five locations, with another under construction, and about 150 employees—and the offers continued to flow, but there were some signs of trouble.

I was on the fence with my adherence to and passion for Mediterranean cuisine. Restaurants were popping up all over Manhattan, and with a dash of olive oil, a spray of fresh herbs, and a few chickpeas, they were calling themselves Mediterranean. It was becoming a saturated market overnight, and it seemed that change might need to be on the horizon for this company to be sustainable. It seemed that my stardom was more like a meteorite—bright for a moment, but fading almost as quickly as it had come.

TRUFFLED MACARONI AND CHEESE

Just like any gourmet recipe, comfort food benefits from the use of impeccable ingredients. Mac 'n' Cheese jumps from good to great when utilizing some of the world's finest provisions: the famous raw milk cheese, fontina val d'aosta, from Alpine Pastures; a high quality black truffle oil—the real stuff, oil infused with truffles; al dente Italian pasta; and a golden top of buttery brioche crumbs. Serve this bubbling, and let the top start to set before digging into the molten-lava-like wonder below the surface.

DRIFTER

Momentum works in many ways, and in 1997, it was certainly not working in my favor. I'd really only known two things throughout my career: success or obstacles followed by success. I had faced so many odd difficulties, and because I always overcame them quite well, they became part of my flow. Still, the cracks were apparent and growing by the day. Every direction I turned presented me with some obstacle.

My regular yoga practice provided me with a clear and balanced perspective, given the circumstances, and my past experience with challenges being short-lived added to my calm. Still, something was changing. New Yorkers at the time were more into the social vibe than the food. Aside from Nica's, I had never been involved in a project that wasn't directly tied to my love for clean, vibrant, and creative Mediterranean food. This was about to change.

Matthew's was holding its own and chugging along fine. Once I had ceased being involved day to day, the numbers were down a little but respectable. Guests who were used to seeing me there anytime they came were disappointed—a downside to operating a namesake business.

I was in the media daily, but while life appeared good, the reality was very different. Nica's was flat. Bar Anise was packed, but I couldn't get a penny out of Selim. Monzu was questionable as it had never been able to generate that "hip factor" a Soho location needed. And most daunting of all, the Grand Central Station restaurant, Metrazur, was nearly $3 million over budget! What started as the opportunity of a lifetime was now a train wreck. Eventually, Metrazur fell apart, and there was no going back for me. Two years of work had basically been lost, but we received a settlement that at least partially compensated us for our time.

Before the train crash, though, the first shoe to drop was Bar Anise.

When Selim refused to pay my percentage-based fee, we went to court and obtained an injunction requiring that he change the name of the restaurant immediately. I didn't own the lease, but our agreement gave me control of the name and trademark of Bar Anise. He refused, of course, so the marshal showed up to forcibly remove the awning.

Meanwhile, it became obvious that Monzu was never going to reach its goals, and we considered closing. I knew the lease was valuable, and instead of closing, suggested we sell the restaurant. Word got around, and the offers were tremendous. We could nearly recapture our entire investment based on the various formal numbers being presented to us. I didn't let that slow us down on other fronts, though.

During a photo shoot for *Vogue* magazine at Monzu, I identified our new direction for that location. I was in my chef coat, stirring a pot of risotto in a kitchen on set with Brazilian supermodel Gisele Bündchen, her arm draped over my shoulder. The photographer, wearing eyeliner and a lopsided hat, was none other than Stephen Meisel, at the time the world's most sought-after man behind the lens. Given his history of shooting every major magazine's covers with the hottest people on the planet, I fully expected this shoot to require all sorts of props and several hours of angles and takes. Instead, he waved his arms around a few times, asking us to shift positions, commented to his assistant, and stepped back from us. *Snap-snap-snap.* We were done.

I noticed a casually dressed, unshaven industry friend standing in the front of the restaurant with a couple of his friends.

"What's up, MK?" John McDonald was an up-and-coming young entrepreneur in NYC; he had all the right contacts, great instincts, and knew Soho. He also had a proposition. He not only wanted to take over the Soho restaurant, but also suggested that Boyd and I could stay involved. It would not be Mediterranean, but would allow us to save some face and hopefully, one day, capture some profit.

Like many things in those days, life changed fast. In a matter of days, John and I hammered out a deal to convert the concept. We closed Monzu, took on a new investment group, and relaunched under a new name—Canteen—with a new design and menu. John spearheaded the concept, and our team managed the business. I was heartbroken over losing Monzu and upset that it was not appealing to the general public despite the dedication we'd spent on researching and developing the cuisine.

John's concept was well-done comfort food, and although it was the last thing I'd want to put in my body, I understood the rationale. There was a backlash in the city against fussy, and cool-comfort was where things were headed. I began to shut down my passionate and creative brain and put on a businessman's hat for a time. I still recall scribbling the menu on a napkin that summer weekend in Maine. It is telling that I can still recite 90 percent of the menu from Malvasia verbatim, but I have to dig very deep to remember anything about Canteen's unremarkable dishes:

1. Roasted Chicken Pot Pie
2. Grafton Cheddar Mac and Cheese
3. Spit-Roasted Chicken Cobb Salad
4. Barbecued Salmon
5. Rice Pudding

Hal Rubenstein, *New York Magazine*'s restaurant critic, summed up our new place quite succinctly:

> When the fifties ended, so did my mother's love of turquoise (though never her need to mambo). The sixties ushered in a new house, and a new kitchen, this time done in too-rich brown and terrifyingly brilliant orange. Canteen's furniture mimics these hues with Twilight Zone precision. When you consider the architectural one-up-yours-manship of many of the spaces just within Manolo distance (and that ain't far), Canteen appears startlingly unfinished.
>
> Yet that may be the very reason it is packed with young people who look far more comfortable here than they do elsewhere. Once you settle into one of those amazing chairs, there is absolutely nothing intimidating about Canteen. Its big, thick, unadorned cream support columns; bare walls; and matching uncovered, unlit ceiling resemble an unfinished basement, minus the hot-water heater in the corner. How, or why, would you put on airs in this space? No wonder everyone looks so relaxed.[4]

He was lukewarm on the food, but it didn't matter. Canteen was packed to the rafters daily. We went from generating $40,000 on a good week at Monzu to more than $125,000 a week at Canteen—nearly a 300 percent increase with the same or lower overhead. Canteen was printing money, and our investors were happy. It was an odd awakening for me to realize I was making money doing something I cared very little about. I wasn't into the nightlife, wasn't into the food, and wasn't excited about much at all. Still, making money wasn't bad for a change.

In the meantime, I had taken over Nica's from Andre and converted it into Café M, with a new design and menu, making a feeble attempt at installing a French Mediterranean concept. No more than a couple months after the conversion—after I'd spent close to $100,000 to change the furniture and rebrand it—I received a letter, a notice of termination, which was the landlords' right if they sold the hotel. I would be kicked out in ninety days, stuck with the bills, our staff would lose their jobs, and we would lose our investment and, as with Metrazur, our time.

I walked into their Midtown office and only the real estate partner was there. I explained my position—we had invested a tremendous amount of money and time into the hotel, and it wasn't fair that we would lose all that. He just looked at me and shrugged.

"I'll have no option other than to take legal action," I threatened.

He pretty much brushed me off with a one-liner:

"I'll call you on Monday."

I've done some of my best work on weekends, and that weekend I poured myself into a new area of expertise. The Internet was just catching on as the best research tool, and it became invaluable to me in this case. I came across a legal term called *detrimental reliance* that I thought could be a basis for our case. Even in the absence of a contract, if one party was damaged due to their reliance on another party's representations, the other party could be found liable for any damages incurred.

I was confident in my newfound information. "Sue them for detrimental reliance," I suggested.

My attorney looked this up and shook his head, a few different expressions crossing his face as he read: he looked amused, then incredulous, then maybe a bit impressed at my audacity.

A few days later, we received our settlement offer: $999,999. I would have to remove all claims and rights to the property and be out in thirty days, but I'd take it. They obviously felt like this settlement was a drop in the bucket compared to losing the $80 million sale to Hyatt.

By the time this settlement closed, we were printing money at Canteen, and we were able to launch a new restaurant, Commune, which took off like a rocket ship.

Commune was an amped-up Canteen—bigger, louder, darker—and instead of just plain old mac and cheese, we had "Truffled Mac 'n' Cheese" and a fried chicken dish named after our publicist's mother. P. Diddy, J.Lo, Ivana Trump, and countless others descended on the place within minutes, and voilà, we had the two hottest restaurants in town.

The press, however, had begun turning on me, as some of the reviews clearly demonstrated.

> Matthew Kenney's Commune may be scalded by its own heat.
>
> Imagine the scene. These clever guys—a sort-of-famous chef and a social wrangler—have a hit hangout in SoHo called Canteen. Now they've snagged a restaurant space in the photo district/Silicon Alley. What to call it?
>
> "Give me a word with seven letters that starts with C," says one.
>
> "Cocoon."

> "That's six letters, idiot."
>
> "Cartoon."
>
> "That's just asking for it. I got it. We'll call it Commune."
>
> "But everyone will be thinking Haight-Ashbury and tie-dye."
>
> "We won't let them think. We'll say it's a tavern for the commune-ity. Get it?"
>
> We're getting it. Commune is not about food. It's barely about dinner, though when he clicks, Matthew Kenney can do wonders . . .[5]

Gael Greene was only one of many reviewers who had similar sentiments. I had traded my creative passion for Mediterranean cuisine to become a scene maker.

Even with the poor reviews, we signed a deal to open a second Commune in Atlanta and another book deal, *Big City Cooking.*

Our company was fragmented now—building great revenue but lacking a clear focus, other than becoming known for creating scenes. I wasn't happy, and although I was still working extremely hard, I had lost that bounce in my step, the reason for rising at 6 a.m. I resorted to practicing a lot of yoga, reading, watching films, and visiting art galleries; I was no longer finding my creative expression in the work I was doing, so I looked for that passion elsewhere. I recall complaining to a friend about not enjoying anything about my profession.

"You have a dream job and a dream life. So many people would love to be in your shoes."

That may have been true, but it simply wasn't for me. Still, I had endured the closing of three restaurants and the loss of another before it even began. Life looked great on paper, great on balance sheets, and even good in the media. What could have been a debacle ended up making me look like a savvy businessman. I came out of a potential quagmire period in better shape than before, and while I no longer loved my work, I had learned the value of perseverance and positivity.

From then on, though, things began to blossom again. On a regular basis, I was featured in *Harper's Bazaar*, *Glamour*, and many other food magazines. *W Mag* followed me up to Maine to see me with my dad, who was monitoring construction on my newest project, The Nickerson Tavern.

We had purchased and renovated The Nickerson Tavern, the only good restaurant in my hometown when I was growing up, and we'd made extensive progress during the summer.

We were also close to launching a new restaurant called Commissary in Portland, Maine. It was a hybrid of Commune and Canteen, but it took a much more respectful approach to food. The restaurant was packed nightly, and I loved my short trips to Maine to visit both new locations. This breather outside of New York took some of the never-ending pressure off my back, and for the first time in a long time, I felt at home.

VODKA MARTINI

In times of distress, we don't remember what we ate because very little brings us joy. We may even forget to eat altogether. If a chilled martini comes to mind, though, it is likely just what the doctor ordered. Splash the cold martini glass with dry vermouth, giving the alcohol one shake before releasing it into the glass with a twist of lemon. Sip and relax.

WRECK

Surviving what seemed like three battles and a war gave me confidence and only further fueled my shift in focus from passionate foodie toward aggressive entrepreneur. Along with our restaurants, we launched a number of other projects, and in those days, I was always game for more.

The place where it all started, Matthew's, continued to be the barometer for everything, and the storm readings weren't looking good. But I didn't want to see the signs. I had spent a few days in Portland, Maine, working on our new restaurant design and organizing our team up there before driving back late one winter Sunday morning. Overall, I'd fooled myself into feeling pretty good about things. Commune and Canteen were booming, Matthew's and Mezze seemed to be holding their own, and our new projects would bring a whole new level of excitement to the company. By the time Atlanta and Maine would open, only a thread of our Mediterranean influence would remain, but I convinced myself that this new way was the best way.

I always loved the drive from Southern Maine to New York City, but about halfway through this particular drive, a call came in on my cell phone from the director of the Maine restaurant.

"Matthew, it's Ted. They said they tried to call you. One of your restaurants in New York had a fire."

My phone hadn't rung, but my cell signal was bad, so it was lucky Ted had been able to reach me at all. The fire was at Matthew's. It began to snow, blanketing my windshield as the late afternoon darkness set in. I called my wife. Kirsten was crying and extremely upset. Matthew's was like a child to her.

"Matthew, it's bad."

She put my attorney on the phone, and he seemed to be more in control. He explained that the damage was extensive, and we would be closed indefinitely. I asked that they secure the place and said we would meet in the morning.

They say you should never fall in love with your business, but why not? I say if you don't love your business, you are not alive. I loved Matthew's—not its physical being, but the energy created when passion meets talent and the product meets guests who just love what you offer them.

Tears covered my face as if the snow were filtering in through the windows until, eventually, I let go. A couple hours later, as I approached the corner of 61st and 3rd for perhaps the ten-thousandth time, the once-glowing globe on the corner was pitch black. Plywood and plastic covered several windows that had been smashed by the firefighters in anticipation of the blaze in the ceiling, the product of an electrical fire. I slowed down for a moment and kept going. Just as the taxi cab had done nearly eight years earlier, this fire closed another chapter. It was time for Matthew's to move on.

My plan was simple. I would not only use the $1 million insurance settlement toward rebuilding Matthew's, but also budget another $500,000, expecting that this would result in a shiny, new operation that we would call Commissary. It would be the sister to our new restaurant in Portland, Maine. With Commune NY and Atlanta, Canteen, and Commissary NY and Maine, Mezze would be the only place standing from the old regime. The change seemed natural, and it promised to position the company for a solid future.

Then things in both my personal and professional life began shifting at a rate so fast my head spun. My ten-year marriage was ending as my wife and I found ourselves living different lives, despite having so much in common and building our New York life together. It was a heartbreaking experience to see our small family, which included three cats and a house, come apart, but it needed to happen. On top of the divorce, our beloved older cat, Bunchy, was not well and had to be put to sleep, and I felt I'd lost everything.

I moved into Sig's apartment on the Upper East Side, and a few months later, I moved into my new girlfriend Sarma's, apartment in the West Village. We had met while she was testing recipes for a new cookbook I was writing at the time, and while it seemed we had very little in common, we formed an unusual bond. I was apparently her favorite chef, and we were both Virgos. Aside from that, it's hard to say what brought our relationship to the surface.

One night, after a few hours of testing recipes at Commune, we had cocktails at the buzzing bar. I recall introducing her to Al, my wise counsel, who never held back his opinions.

"That one is trouble," he said after she left. "Watch out."

I brushed that off as Al being a little envious of my very attractive new friend. The same week, my street-savvy New York publicist met her, as well.

"Be careful of this one; she gonna knife you in the back when you turn around."

Jealous, of course, I told myself. I'd later wish I'd listened to these warnings, but what can I say? Love is blind.

Sarma's birthday fell shortly after mine. I had just turned thirty seven, and life seemed pretty solid. On September 10, 2001, we celebrated her birthday with a nice meal and a bit too much wine at Tom Colicchio's new restaurant, Craft.

I woke a bit later than usual the next morning and rushed to get downstairs to catch a cab to the Upper East Side; I planned to hit my office and then check on the construction progress at Commissary. It was warm for September and a bit hazy and bright. There were normally only a couple people waiting for cabs, but today there was a crowd, maybe twenty people milling about. I was frustrated about the wait I had in front of me. People were agitated, and at first all I noticed was the pacing. Then I registered the alarm on people's faces. I asked a bystander what was going on.

"A plane hit the World Trade Center."

I looked up, since we were not far from Wall Street, and saw a small fire near the top of one of the towers. It seemed like a small plane, and the fire seemed contained.

I called Sarma to let her know about it. "You need to see this—you won't believe what happened."

Soon, she joined me downstairs and we stared at the building for a while until finally deciding that the news on television would offer more insight. Before we could make it upstairs, we heard gasps from the crowd on the ground. The other tower let out an enormous fireball that looked like a bomb. At this point, both towers were on fire and there was confusion everywhere. Terrorism had never crossed our minds at this point.

Within an hour, the lives of so many would be forever changed. The news suspected terrorism, as these were not small planes but rather jets that had been deliberately flown into the towers. A third had crashed in rural Pennsylvania and another had hit the Pentagon. We were bracing ourselves for an all-out war.

The entire area around the towers was decimated by smoke, debris, death, and destruction. People by the hundreds walked north, past our building, to get away from the chaos and to fight for survival. The next several days were a parade of fire trucks, ambulances, and constant news of more threats. The death toll was in the thousands, and tragically, this included Kirsten's sister. New York was on its knees, and the Twin Towers were only the first of many things to come crashing down that year.

Large parts of the city were cut off from traffic, and moving around was next to impossible. We began having conference calls with our managers to coordinate how to take care of our business and employees. Business plummeted, and although many savvy operators would lay off staff, I did not. Still, revenue dropped as much as 80 percent in our larger restaurants, and soon, my company was in serious financial trouble.

We had gone from running powerhouse operations and a growing company to having trouble meeting payroll, much less other expenses. In the space of less than a year, I had transitioned from a major operator to the subject of gossip columns questioning the viability of my company. In order to continue construction of the new Commissary and to stave off some of the mounting debt, I sold my interest in Canteen.

By then, I was accustomed to survival, and at first, I expected things to come around as they always had. Commissary NY opened several weeks after 9/11 and was likely the first major restaurant to do so around this time. The regulars who'd kept Matthew's humming for so many years were nowhere to be found within two months of Commissary's opening. We started off like a rocket but plummeted even faster, going from $17,000 in revenue a day to about $300—no one was walking through the door. And then, adding insult to injury, the reviews came. Some were truly revealing in regard to the turn my career had taken. William Grimes, the *New York Times* food critic, summed it up pretty well:

> Matthew Kenney is really two chefs. The first one cares about good food and has an adventurous, roving eye for unusual ingredients and flavors, usually Mediterranean, that he uses to modernize bistro dishes. This is the Matthew Kenney who delighted diners at Matthew's and challenged them at Monzù, his somewhat wobbly ramble through the cuisines of Sicily and Sardinia.
>
> The second Matthew Kenney is the attractive, socially fluent chef who spends as much time working the dining room as he does working the stove. This Matthew Kenney is the one who signed his name to glib, facile hot spots like Canteen, which he has left, and Commune—restaurants where the design came first, the scientifically planned parties second, and the food third, at best.[6]

In good fighting spirit, I blasted Mr. Grimes with a three-page letter ripping his theory to shreds, and he, wisely, responded and stood by his review. In hindsight, of course, he was not only right but also was being kind. I was a chef who'd gone off the rails of passion into some undefined land.

Then, everything fell apart. We closed Mezze. The catering team became frustrated with my financial problems, and the entire team left to start a new business. My marketing director left to form her own firm. My landlords in Maine got wind of all my problems in New York, and both Commisary Maine and the construction on Nickerson Tavern closed soon after. The project in Atlanta, such a beautiful design, was left in the hands of my partner there and had little to do with me other than in spirit. Commune was for sale, and while I had a signed deal to sell it to TV chef and old friend Bobby Flay for over a million dollars, it was at this time I met the slick Jeffrey Chodorow, founder of China Grill and Asia de Cuba.

I learned later that Chodorow had served time for bankruptcy fraud related to the defunct Braniff airlines, but he also had a big fat bank account and loved to spend money on building restaurants. One food writer described him as "reptilian." I liked him instantly—he was very pleasant and one of the brightest people I'd ever met. Yet there was a detachment in his personality that was both appealing and troubling. When he offered to buy Commune, I couldn't resist.

A year later, he signed a lease for Commune without paying me a dime. He pulled the classic "bleed them dry" trick—string someone along until they can no longer stay in the game, and then eat them. He kept promising to buy Commune, but he came up with one excuse after another, avoiding my calls for weeks at a time. When I finally ran up enough arrears with my landlord to match my cash security deposit, which was nearly $225,000, I walked away, not owing the landlord a dime. Chodorow signed a new lease the same day.

Around the same time, Commissary NY finally gave in. I had no sources of revenue and only mounting bills. I was toasted. When Con Edison disconnected the power at Commissary and I did not have enough money to reconnect it, my staff walked out. I still remember that gorgeous New York afternoon, walking into the store one last time, collecting nothing other than a few personal items, and locking the door for the last time. I was officially out of business.

The headline of the full page article in the *New York Post*, although full of inaccurate statements, summed it up: "Chef's Goo$e is Cooked."

The article began, "Chef Matthew Kenney, whose culinary empire was once the envy of the industry . . . " I was finished.

All that was left was my office, despite the fact it had no power, which meant no phones, fax, Internet, or electricity. I returned to the office for at least two weeks afterward, trying to make sense of what had happened, either answering or ignoring the frequent buzzer, a sure sign of one of many creditors at the door. Finally, I left that key behind as well, and left that phase of my life for good.

BRAZIL NUT MILK

They're often the last ones left in the bowl, but when fresh, these gems have abundant flavor and the perfect fat content for creating a liquid base or a milk to drink on its own. Soak the nuts to improve digestion and make processing easier, then blend them with filtered water for two minutes and strain the mixture through a fine cheesecloth. Enrich the creamy milk with coconut butter, fresh vanilla bean, Himalayan salt, and raw honey. Chill it well. Brazil nut milk makes the best smoothie on the planet when blended with fresh fruit and even cacao.

VEGAN

When we are open to growth and new experiences, they will often appear in the form of opportunities, and then it's up to us to embrace or reject them—a choice I faced during my self-imposed hiatus. I assumed it would be easier to rebuild my lost career than to reinvent myself and my company, but fate wasn't going to have that. When I finally let go and accepted that I'd made poor business choices and that my previous path was a dead-end road, a new path began to form, albeit a winding path full of surprises.

My first surprise came from Rob Matzner. Rob and I first met at Matthew's. He was a colorful, intense man and wiry, not only physically, but also in his tight demeanor. Everything Rob did was at 200 mph—including the motorcycle racing hobby he took up shortly after seeing my canary yellow Ducati. Rob had struggled with addictions and all the ups and downs that come with it, so it wasn't a complete surprise when I learned he was on this wacky new plan called the Raw Food Diet.

Sarma and I had made casual dinner plans with him, and I made a reservation for us at Jean-Georges Vongerichten's hot new French-Chinese restaurant, 66 in Tribeca. Late on a Sunday, the day before our scheduled date, Rob called to inform us that he would like to change the location of our dinner.

"I am eating only raw food right now and would prefer we instead go to a restaurant called Quintessence. It is near your apartment, on 10th Street."

We were more baffled than disappointed. I didn't know much about raw food diets. I had glanced at one article about a chef in San Francisco, a very odd-looking dude with long hair wearing a midriff, who lived on the stuff and claimed it was like having superpowers. (*Scott Pilgrim vs. The World* [2010] parodied that very idea.) It caught my attention, but not enough to read the article in which he was featured with a big bunch of carrots and other raw vegetables. So, with lots of curiosity and very little expectation, we headed out to subject ourselves to the superpower experience firsthand.

I'd lived with Sarma on 10th Street for over a year and must have walked past Quintessence dozens of times without ever noticing it. Not once. It was a shoebox of a place, perhaps fourteen seats in a little cube-shaped room, with a counter for food to be expedited or picked up for take-out. It had the "early-days raw food restaurant" aroma: a slightly spicy, arid, dried-herb vibe that felt healthy but not the least bit appetizing. The room was bare bones: some generic wood and natural tones, more like something I would have tried for a rice bowl in the early '90s. I can't recall if there was music. And most disappointing, Quintessence did not serve wine. So I felt we were pretty much set up to have a brutal evening of flavorless organic vegetables, some seeds, and a nice glass of fermented barley.

Once settled in, I noticed that the small room was actually full, populated by a youthful collection of glowing faces, flush with oxygen and life force as if they had all just stepped out of a bikram yoga class.

Rob carefully explained the philosophy behind raw food; that cooking destroys enzymes and nutrients that are essential to our body's ability to heal itself. This meant only consuming plants—fruits, vegetables, nuts, seeds, and sprouted grains. Foods that were still alive. Setting science aside, it made some sense. Food that is alive would nourish our bodies and minds. Then again, I already ate plenty of salads and good doses of lean proteins, and never too much sugar or caffeine or alcohol, so I didn't think this fad diet would make much of a difference.

We sat next to a pretty young woman from Staten Island, Danielle, who went on and on about the magic of raw food. Rob ordered for us all—something called Peter's Pot (which reminded me a little of witch's brew), a few Mexican-inspired dishes, a couple salads, and desserts that had the pasty, dense texture of nuts pureed with dates. If it hadn't been for the glowing, healthy bodies filling the room, or the conversation—which, despite seeming a bit hyped, intrigued me—this would likely have been a one-off for me, maybe even a battle scar. I wanted wine. I wanted flavor. I wanted fewer onions and food that was balanced by the deft hand of a trained chef. And I definitely wanted to be in a sexier dining room.

Unlike most dinner conversations, ours that night focused entirely on the benefits of raw food. At first, I wondered whether everyone was simply reassuring each other to comfort their eating disorders. Then again, they mentioned an eccentric guy in San Francisco who was doing some pretty progressive stuff with raw food and a woman in Marin County who had turned it into an art form. Something amazing was happening to the raw food scene from the sound of things, and even this mediocre meal left us feeling incredible.

A typical restaurant meal makes you feel tired, a bit heavy or bloated, ready for a cab ride home and instant sleep. Rob jumped in his Range

Rover to head back to the Upper East Side, but Sarma and I were so full of energy that we decided to walk up around Gramercy Park, down Fifth Avenue, and all over on that gorgeous summer night while we talked about the experience, both of us noting how energized we felt. Despite thousands of NYC restaurant meals over the years, I'd only experienced this feeling once before, after an ethereal meal at the Soho soba restaurant, Honmura An. Although it was after 10 p.m., we came home to 4th Avenue and immediately went online to read up on raw food. It seemed like the West Coast was where things were happening. One look at the website of Roxanne's, the Larkspur, California, restaurant opened by Roxanne Klein, and the light bulb switched on for good.

I knew it then and there—this food, produced at a high level by professional chefs, served in a contemporary, comfortable setting with organic wine (wine is raw!), would revolutionize food. The passion I had felt nearly fifteen years ago when rifling through cookbooks, coming home at midnight to prepare risotto, and peering in restaurant windows was a distant memory. Yet, despite being absent from my life for more than a decade, and despite recently being beaten down beyond submission, the fire returned instantly. I couldn't stop searching and printing and reading, couldn't think about anything other than how potentially explosive it would be if someone could make healthy food cool.

This initial euphoria was dimmed a bit when I woke up. I was trained to cook food and had built whatever foundation I had on my upbringing, classical training, and experience preparing food with heat, and by utilizing animals throughout. Family traditions were non-existent without this classic cuisine, holidays were built around it, and what about my passion for Maine lobster? Where would I get protein? I didn't want to become a skinny vegan.

Fad diets come and go, but we were curious enough to walk over to 10th Street between A and B to find a place called Jubb's Longevity, a hidden East Village fountain of youth that, supposedly, sold the best nut milks on the planet. Until Rob pushed us into going, I didn't even recognize nut milk as a real food.

If Quintessence felt a bit fringe, Jubb's took it to a whole new level. We found the little four-hundred-or-so-square-foot storefront on a dingy block, with a plain blue awning and a bench out front with a couple of characters having some kind of smoothie. A smoothie made with the magical nut milk, I presumed. It reminded me of one of those below-ground apartments in the Village that you can peer into from the street: inside there always seems to be a couple tall plants still in their plastic pots and a random chair and table in the middle of the room. The wall of Jubb's was filled with supplements and books, the right side had a counter with some refrigerated food and a cashier, and there was a small kitchen in the back. There were posters and signs and things all around this place, but two details captured all my attention.

Even in the East Village, you can't help but take notice of an older man, maybe sixty years old, lean and fit, with his hair up in a bun on top of his head, tied up in some contraption where he threaded strands through multi-colored beads. This all went nicely with his five or six necklaces, a mixture of crystals, some turquoise, and a few symbols. A skin-tight, black, long-sleeved cotton t-shirt with a low-cut neck was pasted to his lean body, the bottom ending about two inches above the tight jeans he had pulled up to his belly button. This guy wasn't doing anything subtle. A plastered grin, all teeth, emanated out from behind the counter when he wasn't barking instructions at a couple of shop hands trying to put orders together for the few customers in the place. This was going to be interesting.

"How are you?" his heavily accented Australian voice warmly asked. He had a nurturing, thoughtful presence. "I'll be right with you."

I read the menu board on the wall behind the cash register—brazil nut milk, almond milk, superfood smoothie, blue-green algae smoothie, life-food casserole, not-salmon pâté. It was innocent-enough stuff, although the food in casserole dishes in the deli case looked tired, nothing was green, and there were a bunch of simply packaged, dried-out niblets in baggies on the counter. Next to the niblets, in front of the cash register, I noticed a fuzzy photograph.

The plexiglass framed eight-by-ten was leaning against the register and showed what looked like a pile of semisoft, light green moon rocks. There were similar pictures behind the register. I'd heard at dinner that this guy, Jubb, was not only a vegetarian, not only a vegan and raw foodist, but also a living "breatharian," a wise man that lived on air. At first glance, I thought there may have been some weeds involved in that formula, as well.

"What is this photo?" I asked, and mentioned our friend Rob sent us to see him for nut milks.

With excitement, he started barking at the assistants to prepare samples. He handed us a cup of thick, cold, delicious brazil nut milk, seasoned with honey, vanilla, and sea salt, and fortified with coconut butter. This blew my mind. The treats kept coming. We tried a mix of dehydrated, seasoned seeds with a bit of a teriyaki flavor, wrapped in crispy nori, and we really liked it. The food was weird, but well-seasoned—much better than anything I'd tried the night before.

Once he finished feeding us, he brought our attention back to the picture. "Gallstones, mate. These were quite a cultivation . . . these here, also." He indicated to all the photos behind the cash register.

Jubb proceeded to explain the basis for his notorious gallstone cleanse, liver flush, parasite treatment, and all the other remedies he had up his sleeve to cure the human race from its diseases. He shared information readily and warmly—in fact, he was quite the host, although digging a bit deeper, we found that each of these cleanses required six or ten of his "supplements" and really could only be consumed with his beverages, foods (mostly simple-looking $20 portions of casseroles or wraps), or $12 smoothies without any fresh fruit or vegetables in them. In fact, what I noticed most about this place was that there were no fresh vegetables or greens in sight. Instead, it was filed with powders, potions, dried herbs, and spices, and it felt a bit more like a laboratory than a kitchen, albeit one I'd still be willing to eat from. It was clean, just bizarre.

"Rob has leaky gut," Jubb told me before launching into an explanation of the colon and something about bowel movements.

This guy had mastered the art of selling food—speak about subjects that are so uncomfortable for the general public, they'll buy food just to reconnect with reality. We picked up a few little items, including his "cook" book, *Lifefood*, and took a deep breath at the $80 bill we ran up for a few trinkets and nibbles.

"See you, mate," he called as he went back to the kitchen like a whirling dervish.

We headed toward home with another detour planned on the way, a stop at a little underground raw food emporium located in the same three-block radius. This one, High Vibe, was in the basement of a residential building, accessible through a buzzer and a walk through the main lobby and down a steep set of outdoor stairs, which landed us in a low-ceilinged old room. This place was orderly and filled with books, some snacks, a bunch of supplements, and things like aloe juice, cleanse packs, cookies called "raw-eos," and tons of powders and pills and nuggets of life force. And yet again, no greens, no fresh fruit—nothing to eat.

One final stop was Live Live—not pronounced *liv liv* or *lahyv lahyv*, but *liv lahyv*. Let the experts figure that one out. This store was the nicest of them all, clean and organized, with many of the same books and products as High Vibe, but with a friendlier vibe, as the place was presided over by a tall, soft-spoken gentleman named Christopher.

Imagine: four businesses devoted to the raw vegan lifestyle within four blocks of our home, and we'd never heard of any of them. What else might be out there? I couldn't wait to crack into this mystery world and, even more importantly, to make my mark on it.

HEIRLOOM TOMATO LASAGNA

Rethink pasta: thinly slice summer squash—brush with olive oil, season with sea salt and fresh oregano leaves—layer with oily pistachio pesto, raw tomato sauce (made rich with bright red sundried tomatoes), a savory, creamy puree of macadamia nuts, and wedges of green zebra tomatoes. Top with even more herbs and green olive oil and present it delicately. You won't miss the traditional version; let's proclaim a new king.

VISIONARY

New Yorkers always believe they are on the cutting edge, but something told me that wasn't the case with the whole raw food "movement." Very little seemed to be moving—if anything, it was good material for a parody after *Sex and the City* featured it on a recent episode. It would be impossible to sustain a normal lifestyle by relying on the places Rob had told me about—one can't live on powders and seeds, after all—and there didn't seem to be any indication of more happening in the city. If it weren't for reading about Roxanne's, I probably would have taken a lot longer to come around. Still, she had no cookbooks published, and at the time, I couldn't afford a plane ticket anywhere, so imagination was pretty much all that was at my disposal.

A week or so went by, and we alternated our traditional food with some raw food, mostly ordering in from Quintessence or picking things up from Jubb's. I didn't really try to make anything at that time—I felt it would be easy to outdo what I'd seen, but I didn't have the tools or the time to think about it. In those days, it wasn't about flavor, but rather how it made me feel. Digestion was one of the first things I noticed after the energy boost. Nobody wants to talk about it, but so much of the world is bloated, gassy, and full of undigested food. This raw stuff went through me like a bullet, which made me feel like I was as light as a feather, not to mention healthier, sexier, and clearer.

After some investigation, there were signs of light in the raw scene—I heard about this place on Ludlow Street, on the fringe of the Lower East Side, called Organic Avenue. They held raw food events, sold hemp clothing, and brought in green coconuts and the occasional durian. This went on a few days a week, sort of like an underground co-op.

While it had the same odd products as the other places, the operators of Organic Avenue, a young couple, were a little more polished than the rest of the crew I'd met. Doug seemed to be the brains behind the business, a fast-talking slickster who would get you so excited about the green coconuts that you'd empty your wallet just to take one home with you. He was passionate and closely connected to the raw food prophet, David Wolfe. I'd heard of Wolfe's speeches about aliens and other abstract subjects, but he also had some very well-written books on the subject of raw food that broke down the reasoning behind the movement a bit more successfully. Doug's partner was Denise, a beautiful, glowing blonde. Her energy was a bit elusive, though her eyes were like nothing I'd ever seen. Sarma and I began to call her "clear eyes," as she embodied that glowing look so many of the raw foodists had.

At one seminar held by Organic Avenue, we experienced a breakthrough dinner by a chef, Chad Sarno. It was miles above anything I'd tried; he apparently had worked with Roxanne. We also met a woman who claimed to have cured inoperable cancer with her diet and lifestyle, along with cleansing, and we met many others who had overcome all sorts of health challenges, succeeded in weight loss, or simply found that their lives were blossoming when following this path.

No doubt that some of these wonderful people were a bit flaky. I knew that some of the stories about raw food were a bit exaggerated—one person claimed he could get ripped lying on the couch simply because of his raw diet, and others talked about changing their hair color back from gray. This is where Rob's genius came in. If anyone else had introduced me to raw food, I probably wouldn't have batted an eye, but Rob was a hard-nosed businessman, an athlete, and he simply didn't mess around or waste time with things that did not deliver results. He recognized something within this world, and following his cue, so did I. My heart still lived and breathed the culinary industry and food, and I saw no alternative: I would bring together this newfound avenue toward optimum health with my beloved profession.

Obesity had already begun skyrocketing, both in adults and youths. Onset diabetes in teens was reaching record levels. The cost of healthcare attributed to weight-related diseases was in the trillions; food kills more of us than alcohol, nicotine, and automobiles combined. Although studies were showing us what the cause of these food issues were, and scientific facts were used to tell people what to eat and when, the message kept changing.

The scientists and writers and doctors were missing the most important point—we are pleasure seekers; even animals want food that they believe tastes good. How can we logically expect society to eat something simply because it's good for them? It has to *feel* good. That's where chefs come in.

Perhaps in another, more evolved society, mainstream chefs would be considered drug dealers, doling out delicious morsels of poison that people become addicted to: salt, sugar, meat, fat. As they grow more and more powerful, the funds continue to back them, creating glorious dining halls to house the action. Food television has continued to grow, along with the waistbands of the chefs hosting those shows. Although not true of every chef on television, we have to ask ourselves what kind of society glorifies a 5'8" red-faced chef who, in his thirties, weighs three hundred pounds, consumes copious amounts of food and alcohol, and looks like walking death? Who believes that this person has the skills to prepare something nourishing for our bodies? Would you go to an auto mechanic whose car was broken down outside the repair shop?

With my new diet, little by little, my energy was improving. I began having regular digestion and feeling clearer. If it weren't for physical results, I would have attributed much of this to a placebo effect, but my aches and pains disappeared, and I could run without any issues at all. My cravings for flour and refined sugars went away. We went all in: no caffeine, little to no wine, simply a 100-percent-raw-food diet. I wouldn't even have a piece of chewing gum in those days, and the immediate benefits were clear.

More important than simply understanding what raw food was, I saw how it could improve my life and *why* I should make the switch. We go through life eating what we think we need based on carbohydrates, fats, and calories without understanding the basic functionality of our bodies. As many of our new "raw" friends said, "What you take out of your body is as important as what you put in."

Meats and animal proteins clog up your intestines and take days to properly digest. Meanwhile, plants digest overnight, in twelve hours or so, leaving the body clean and free to rebuild, recharge, and store energy. It's so simple, and yet we've complicated it beyond belief. This *why* is what motivated me to dive headfirst into an exotic new world and not only make it my personal choice but also dedicate my career to it.

The only way to be truly successful in anything is to give it everything. I don't believe in disconnecting my work and my personal preferences—although I allowed that to happen in previous years, I wasn't going to do it again. Certainly, there were easier ways for an educated, healthy, intelligent, and attractive man to make a living than carving a career out of peddling raw food to the unbelievers. The audience at Organic Avenue wasn't going to fill any restaurants with 100 seats and a $50-per-person check average. And yet, I saw it as clear as day: Nobu Matsuhisa had a global empire of multimillion dollar restaurants selling sushi and creative interpretations of Japanese cuisine. We had barely acknowledged sushi in America until a few years ago, and now it was a phenomenon. Not only did I believe raw food could achieve the same level of success, but I felt it could be even bigger—if, and only if, someone could make it delicious and sexy. Then, bringing together health and flavor, people could have the best of both worlds.

With these newfound visions firmly rooted, Sarma and I scheduled a meeting with Jeffrey Chodorow. To move forward, we would need financial support. Though he'd burned me before, Chodorow was always game for discussing new projects. Like myself, he was a deal junkie to the max—my biggest weakness—and despite a tremendously unbalanced set of financial circumstances between us, I communicated as his equal. I didn't trust him, but I had never been so vulnerable and weak professionally. He was really the only one who owed me, so I saw this as a way to get back in the game. I told myself I'd figure out how to protect myself from him later. We dove straight into it, explaining the concept we had in mind: a raw food restaurant built for a mainstream audience with gourmet variations on the hippie cuisine we were seeing around town.

"Everyone is into yoga and health. This is what's trendy now," I explained.

"This is like Roxanne's, in California. I know they do well," he acknowledged. He knew of it; that surprised me. "I've eaten there. It was really good."

Although still sketchy about details, I was encouraged by his last comment.

"Let's look around and see what spaces might work for it."

While the space search was slow-moving, Sarma and I did take steps to equip our kitchen at home with the proper tools and ingredients. This, too, was slow at first given our lack of experience and recipes to go on. A visit to Maine during these early days pretty much summed up what a challenge we had ahead of us. Coconuts were a big part of the raw diet, and although I couldn't find any young Thai coconuts in the town of two thousand where I grew up, I was able to capture one mature brown fuzzy one in the local market.

"How do I open this thing?"

Fifteen minutes later, I stood in the grass with my axe, cracking the thing in half. In all my years as a chef, I'd never opened a coconut. This is a big realization for any chef transitioning from traditional cuisine to raw and whole foods. In a restaurant, even a great restaurant, the chef buys milk; he doesn't have a cow in a back room behind the prep kitchen. In a raw restaurant, we make the milk. It comes from plants or seeds or trees. This coconut became a metaphor for what I was about to embark on: nothing would come easy.

This long weekend in Maine was the first time I'd been "all raw" around my family. We didn't dine together, but we talked about my new way of living. My dad listened and said very little, but my mom was interested. Later, my brother would call me to discuss it.

"Dad says he's worried this raw food stuff is going to make you skinny and sickly."

I experimented with a few dishes that weekend, none of which were edible or attractive. Falling back on classical flavors, I tried to make a concoction resembling meatloaf from walnuts and mushrooms and herbs. It tasted exactly as it sounds. My first shot at making my own Rejuvelac (a fermented drink made from sprouted grains) was moldy and sour. Even more troubling was the grainy hummus made from sprouted chickpeas. It was not just flavorless; it was a literal gas ball. The lesson in all this was that relying on tried-and-true recipes or pairings was useless. I didn't doubt the viability of the vision we had, but I knew it was going to require a massive learning curve.

Back at home in New York, things slowly came together. Relying on Jubb's overly sweet and overly fatty smoothies, I at least began to successfully replace breakfast with something raw and tasty. Lunch was easy, since I'd become comfortable with the high-fat aspect of this diet: lots of nuts and avocado, sea vegetables, and elements such as hemp seeds, which added richness, protein, and flavor. Vinegars are mostly heated, so I relied on citrus. The farmer's market and a Whole Foods store were both close by, so it was easy to work in quality ingredients. Still, I struggled with the gourmet versions—nobody would come to our dream restaurant for an avocado.

One day, after multiple failed attempts at dehydrated delicacies, I decided to fall back on some classics—I'd make a lasagna, with simple pesto, tomato sauce, and a creamy cheese. The thought process was pretty straightforward. Use zucchini in place of flat noodles, season it well, then layer it with herbs and fresh tomatoes and three delicious sauces. The pesto was a slam dunk. Using pistachios instead of pine nuts, the texture was good, and with plenty of salt and olive oil, it wasn't missing the parmesan.

I'd been hearing about nutritional yeast as a good vegan source of B-12, and it was used in a lot of raw packaged products at High Vibe, so I figured that it would give the nuts—in this case, pignoli—a flavor counterpart that could be processed to be like a chunky ricotta. It needed some water and a ton of lemon, but it was pretty good.

The simplest part should have been the tomato sauce—easy enough, and anyone can make tomato sauce, right? Not so fast. I learned the hard way that the concept of reduction (cooking out liquid, thereby intensifying flavor) didn't work without heat. So rather than blending my way to tomato sauce heaven, I resorted to adding in some sun-dried tomatoes, both for a flavor boost and a textural balance. With a hint of chili, fresh oregano, lemon, and a touch of honey, the result was rich and delicious.

I knew this dish would rock because the components all rocked on their own. It was as if a garden in mid-summer landed on a plate. I layered the components—zucchini, fresh tomato, herbs, olive oil, tomato sauce, pesto, "ricotta"—repeated the layering two more times, and ended up with a towering, vibrant-looking stunner representing raw food. It was as flavorful as it was attractive. Finally, a breakthrough.

Then the magic really began to flow. I had finally mastered opening young coconuts: make a three-point hit on the pinnacle of the shaved shell, empty and save the electrolyte-filled water, scoop out the sweet flesh, and it's done. So one night, when my sweet tooth was calling out, coconut answered. In those days, raw cacao powder was not even on the market, so we used roasted cocoa powder. And agave, which has come and nearly gone, wasn't readily available. Still, from young coconuts, cocoa powder, maple syrup, sea salt, and vanilla bean, blended and set, we had pudding. A rich, delicious, sweet-tooth satisfying dessert that had no refined sugar, eggs, dairy, or artificial ingredients whatsoever. Another breakthrough.

My yoga practice intensified, and I was hitting a flow that I'd never found before. In savasana (or "corpse pose") one weekday night, I felt totally clear—my body relaxed and my mind receptive. I had a vision of a dish: shiitake ravioli with asparagus and wild mushrooms. It was out of left field, but I made it, and it stuck. I'd finally found my style.

There was so much work ahead, so many things to figure out. Three dishes don't make a brand; we needed to understand how this food could be produced for larger volume, how long it lasted, what it would cost to make it, how to train people to understand it, and, most importantly, how to make people like it.

Despite all the challenges ahead, it was clear we were on to something, and it needed to be shared. As I was discovering these brilliant flavors, my body was loving every minute of it, my mind and vision was clear, and the professional passion that had been gone for so long was alive and well in my new plant-based world.

CHOCOLATE PUDDING

It's good practice to occasionally abandon tradition. When most people look at a coconut, they see a coconut. Others see pudding. Drink the water and scoop out the milky flesh. Process the coconut flesh well with cacao power, sweeten with maple syrup, hit it with a touch of cinnamon, salt, and vanilla extract, and chill it for a bit. More of us would eat plant-based if we realized how easy and delicious it can be.

SEARCHER

Many months before I discovered raw food, when it was obvious my company wasn't going to survive, I received a letter from the University of Maine notifying me that I had been chosen to receive an award—the annual Spirit of Maine Achievement Award, given to outstanding alumni who have excelled in their careers and communities. While I was flattered to be chosen, I also felt embarrassed to be given this recognition; the nomination came upon the heels of my serious career crash, and I was so far down, I could not even see my way up again yet. I wrote the Alumni Director's office to explain my thoughts on this and suggested that they may want to choose an alternate, since my career was not only in a tailspin, but had crashed, exploded, and burned. While I was working hard to rebuild, I offered to step aside in favor of other candidates.

"Your perseverance and commitment is another reason we would like you to receive this award," they wrote back. "Thank you for being open about this, but we would like you to have it."

I was honored and pleased and looked forward to visiting my alma mater in the fall. Meanwhile, I was searching New York for a venue for my raw foods restaurant.

Everyone who has looked for a location to open a business in New York realizes that the city's major game is real estate, not restaurants. "Location, location, location," my friends. Landlords control what goes where, and most of their decisions are based solely on the rate of return they can realize with their property. I was no longer in the high-budget phase of my career when I could afford, and even command, the best locations. My new budget wasn't even an eighth of what I'd had with Commune, and our concept made eyes roll in those days. One advantage we had was that Chodorow appeared to be throwing money around to open restaurants all over the place. The other possible upside was that raw cooking did not require traditional gas or heat, so fire ventilation would not be required. This would save us a lot of money and also allow us to potentially build in spaces that most restaurants could not. So I hit the pavement on foot, bike, and taxi, scouring the city for our location.

While we shopped locations, our dehydrator at home was running 24/7, working up crackers and cookies and bars and treats as we were experimenting to the max. The Vitamix cranked up the kitchen volume every morning, and our refrigerator—which had once been filled with dairy, fish, bread, and eggs—was now packed to the brim with sprouts, coconuts, greens, and fruit. Our cabinets were stocked with powders, while tons of nuts and seeds and spices and avocados dominated the countertops. Going on a raw food diet automatically cuts down your supermarket visits—and your environmental footprint—by 80 percent. You won't need anything in a can, anything processed, anything from the dairy section, or anything from the meat or fish sections; most boxed and processed foods will be eliminated, including soft drinks. Just focus on the produce section and a few dried or pantry items, and you're all set. It's not as limiting as it sounds, especially when you start to realize how boldly colorful the array of fruits and vegetables is.

We also acquired some pretty cool tools and machines, including a Pacojet, which is an ice cream maker on steroids. Since it both aerates and blends at the same time, we were able to create a fluffy, creamy, ultra-rich ice cream from young coconut, cashews, and other fun ingredients. The bowls of nuts and seeds soaking in water around the kitchen were becoming easier to turn into gourmet dishes, full of color, richness, and intense flavor. The more sophisticated this food became, the more excited we became to share it with the world.

I was feeling better every day. Despite not being financially stable and being under the thumb of Chodorow, I was physically another person entirely. After a few years of less-than-perfect digestion and other minor health-related issues—mostly aches and pains I attributed to getting older—I felt lighter, clearer, and ready to jump out of my own skin. This wasn't a nervous or anxious energy, but simply a vibration so powerful that I felt I had more energy than I needed, the way it must feel to drive a Formula One car on a neighborhood street. Rather than let that excess energy go to waste, I put it into yoga, creative exercises, reading, and the new restaurant project. Although most people don't want to talk about it, there is simply nothing like having a digestive system that processes food like clockwork. You wake up, having completely and fully digested the previous day's meals, and feel like a child again, fresh and clean and full of energy.

I wanted more, to experiment in pushing my health further. In conjunction with raw foods, we hear a lot about cleanses, and while I feel most people overdo them and rob their bodies of the nutrients they need to be strong, there is merit to periodically giving your body a rest and removing impurities. Such was our motivation when Sarma and I decided to try the infamous gallbladder-and-liver cleanse that Dr. Jubb offered.

I don't even recall how we could afford the $400 worth of powders, teas, and potions at the time. The grocery list was insane: olive oil, tons of sea salt, digestive tea, and too many other products to list. After a week of swallowing pills, downing tonics, wrapping my liver in a castor oil pack and plastic wrap, and performing self-induced enemas and colonics, I was finally prepped and ready for the actual gallbladder "flush."

By the time I finished this self-assault, since my body was so wracked from being "cleansed," swollen from the impact of all these foreign substances on my system, red from the niacin flush that was administered each afternoon, and simply starving because I couldn't have solid food, I was actually kind of looking forward to drinking a whole cup of olive oil—the crown-jewel moment of this program. The theory is that once your gallstones are all coagulated due to Jubb's brilliant extraction process—which, of course, is far better than surgery—they are ready to come out; thus the term "flush." All the stones need is some lubrication, and the expensive olive oil he sells will do the trick. After a week of sweating, flushing, peeing, starving, aching, and feeling in general like a dump truck ran over me, I wanted some magic.

Olive oil is like a brother to me; I love it, though drinking a full cup straight doesn't seem quite as appealing as dipping a great piece of crusty bread into an ounce or so of it. A small squeeze of lemon in the whole cup of oil didn't help much as I tried to sip down the monster dose. It took about forty minutes, but I finally got it all down. It was so heavy on my system that I could feel oil coming out of my eyes and fingernails, and it seemed as though someone dropped an anchor into my stomach. I could barely lift my feet, much less make it to yoga class. I thought that this must be what people feel like when they have a little minor cosmetic work done and they like how it looks, so they go for an all-out makeover. They want to make everything just a little bit better, but before they know it, they've gone too far and look like Catwoman. That great buzz I'd been carrying around was a distant memory; instead, I was a skinny vegan slug on a couch.

The stones never appeared, although the oil did work its way through my body, and eventually—about a week later—I felt energetic again. Just remembering that cleanse brings back the nausea. Maybe I needed it, though. I may never know if it was simply the break from solid food or if this hocus-pocus actually worked, but I must admit that my body eventually recovered to a point of purity I have never experienced in my life.

Finally back on my feet after the flush and deep into the planning of my raw food endeavor, I geared up to fly to Maine for homecoming and to accept my award. When I arrived in Orono, the home of the University of Maine, the first thing I did after checking into my low-budget motel was throw on my running clothes and head out to revisit my old college campus. I hadn't seen it in at least fifteen years. Much was the same. My run covered every place I had lived or studied during all my years in Orono. I ran by the stream where our rugby team jumped in the ice-cold river after practice and by the store that sold me beer when I was still underage. But while fast food was still the theme, most of the food joints were now unrecognizable from my days.

On the other hand, Stillwater Village, my home for two years, looked exactly the same. This was where I learned how to do laundry and discovered that I couldn't live in a frat house atmosphere. A few hundred yards down the road, my old wild Signma Nu fraternity house was now an unrelated sorority—a casualty of the more conservative way the campus was running, and probably for the better. The fewer boys who are subjected to that madness, the better the world will be.

Past the old rugby field and the women's gymnasium, and finishing on a high at the end of Greek Row, my knees and joints felt better than they had in years. As I breathed in this fall air, I felt optimistic, like a twenty-year-old who had yet to make plans in the big world. I could see faces and hear voices from years past, and it was a very powerful, moving experience. I accepted the award later that day at halftime during the homecoming game, and the next day I was on my way back to New York.

Back in the big city, I continued searching for a location for our restaurant and continued innovative experimentation with raw food. As I adjusted to an entirely new food paradigm, I was grateful for the chat rooms and blogs that were popping up all over the Internet; they allowed me to keep up with what was happening in the restaurant industry since I wasn't really in touch with anyone outside of my new raw world. I happened to see a comment on one board called *Chowhound* from an employee of a cute little restaurant called Verbena in the Gramercy Park area. She referenced that it might be closing. It was ambiguous, but I was like a ferocious dog with a bone when it came to looking for restaurant spaces.

Verbena was the perfect size and had the best outdoor back garden in the entire city. It would be a dream for us to open there! Since nothing was official, and the restaurant wasn't on the market, we reached out to Chodorow's broker, who quickly tracked down the owner of the building. She was non-committal about what was happening, but said she would take a meeting.

As it turns out, the landlady was vegetarian. (Score!) When we found out that Verbena would be out at the end of the month, I knew we had to take it. Chodorow wasn't sold—gardens didn't impress him, nor did the $20,000-per-month price tag. Moreover, the place was filthy, and there were dozens of dead water bugs everywhere. Grease lined the exhaust hood, and it had that haunted aroma of a long-dead restaurant. It was hard to imagine this once jewel-of-a-place had only closed a week ago. I could see its bones, though—still good and strong and salvageable—and Chodorow used his muscle to get a lease signed. Thus began my second career.

MAKI ROLL

Top crisp nori sheets with a mixture of pulsed jicama root, pine nuts, and rice vinegar—dry to evoke a rice-like fluffiness. Wrap the sheets around generous chunks of avocado, soy-marinated shiitake, asparagus, and tomato. Roll it tight, and the resulting roll is both artful and edible, a clean variation on a classic.

PURIST

New York loves a comeback. As ruthless as it can feel being on the receiving end of a good old-fashioned Manhattan lashing, the way back up can be a truly heartwarming experience. From those few who were there for me during my freefall, to others who disappeared from my circle while I toiled away making flax crackers and raw cookies in obscurity, to some of my harshest critics, most everyone seemed supportive as I worked my way back into the industry.

The new restaurant, Pure Food and Wine, would be the first time in nearly fifteen years that I was involved in a project that could have all my attention. I had no clients, no books being published, and certainly no empire to run. I had less going on than I did when I built Matthew's so many years ago, so it was a real pleasure to give my all to one entity.

Our budget was limited, and although Chodorow and I were both known for doing high-budget projects, we did this one on a shoestring. There were essentially four spaces to design: the kitchen, the garden, the dining room, and the takeaway shop. We started with the best: the garden. I came across a gorgeous photo from one of the Aman Resorts that showed low-slung, cushioned benches surrounding a fire pit. While we were not doing the pit, I thought this would be a unique way to create the warmth of an indoor space outdoors. We could not afford a big-name general contractor, so instead, I hired my college buddy Russell to oversee everything. Russell wasn't your typical spreadsheet-and-timeline kind of guy. This would add a lot of color to the whole experience.

"This is a little loosey-goosey for me, but okay," Chodorow said in response to Russell's messy, nonsensical bids.

He wasn't sure this could work, but something told me it could.

Russell took me to a lumber yard in the Bronx and showed me a dark wood called IPE, which he suggested for the outside. It turned out to be ideal, and we built a large fence all around the perimeter. Rich, chocolate wood and cushioned outdoor banquettes enveloped the entire garden. We left a few feet behind the benches open to plant a pretty little herb garden. Chodorow's beautiful wife, Linda, did the planting, and we sourced some very sexy burgundy and grape fabrics for the benches and chairs.

The dining room was easier: a simple, little, low-ceilinged space with absolutely nothing special about it. It was about the size of the private dining room we had at Commune, nothing more than what I would once have considered a throwaway space. We painted it so many colors before deciding on one we could live with: a Ralph Lauren khaki, then a Martha Stewart light green, an off-white, and finally, the most brilliant red-orange that was so overpowering that it almost felt tacky at first. It somehow worked, though—color can do so much, not only for food, but for design as well.

Then came the furniture. Chodorow had opened and closed so many places recently, he probably had several acres worth of recycled equipment. I remembered some great chairs he had at a restaurant called Tuscan; he'd removed them because they were always breaking. Tuscan was a 300-seat restaurant, and since we only had about fifty seats inside, we would have extras if they broke. We upholstered the chairs in an equally brilliant raspberry red and refinished the dark wood. Sarma found a couple of duck photos she liked that became the only unique element of the décor, aside from the dark wood we clad the walls with.

We got a quote for $25,000 to have a kitchen designer lay out that portion, but we soon realized that we could not afford it, and it didn't matter anyway; a raw kitchen is nothing like a cooking kitchen. Once we removed the hood, we set about creating a space that was designed for this food, our new food, complete with dehydrators and plenty of counter space done in Carrara marble. We also gave the kitchen some warm touches: wood walls, a transposed image of a big Buddha on canvas, and some plants. Just as Matthew's felt like "a coffee table book come to life," Pure Food and Wine had the same spirit, perhaps even more so. It was tied to a more meaningful purpose, so it surely had some angels behind it.

We went through the usual hurdles, moving things around, making adjustments, and even putting up and taking down the ugly awning, but at the end of the day, this place simply embodied beauty and nature. There was a breeze working its way through the dining room as we set up, and with flowers everywhere, there was an element of peace, in part related to the natural fabrics and the lack of leather and heavier elements that usually embody a restaurant design.

The kitchen is the heart of any business, as Gennaro taught me so many years ago. It would be interesting to see what a kitchen was like without the humming of hoods, the snap and crackle of hot oils, the muggy warmth from steaming pots, the intensity that comes with fire, and the realization that you are always one wrong move away from a major burn to your flesh. Everyone kept asking me about this sensual aspect, and in reality, it never concerned me. Most restaurant kitchens smell like oil and grease, and you go home at night with that heavy aroma in your hair and pores—even the freshest fish still takes on a strong aroma when cooked. I wasn't the least bit concerned about leaving all that behind. And, in fact, I was excited to come home not smelling like overdone food and feeling toxic because of it.

We pulled together an interesting kitchen team: Sarma and me, plus three sous chefs who would split duties managing food production. It wasn't easy teaching what was so new and dear to us to cooks who had never seen or tasted this imaginary food before, but it came together day by day. I knew it was the future of food the moment we finally took possession of the kitchen Russell built. As I would later write in my journal:

> The first time I stepped into a raw food kitchen, I knew I had discovered something magical. My senses had been on high alert, as I remained deeply suspicious about uncooked food, and many years in professional kitchens had created a foundation of principles contrary to what I was about to experience. Yet, I nearly became an instant convert, ready to forgo not only fire and heat, but also the majority of ingredients that were the building blocks of my cuisine.
>
> To this day, I still remain captivated by steaming pots of risotto, the hearty aromas of a wood-fired oven, and the intense flavor brought on by a long-simmering reduction. Yet, nothing has ever captivated my attention in a kitchen like the crisp smell of fresh ginger, mingling with coriander and lime, as I entered that day. And nothing has held it like the explosive clean flavor of raw organic foods.[7]

It had been years since I felt this way: attached to the food in a passionate way, with little more motivating me than a desire to create a path and to share it with the world. In the earlier days of my career, I was never motivated by money or empire building, but rather, the desire to bring guests an experience that moved me, hoping it would do the same for them. This was also true with raw food. I had answered one of contemporary life's greatest riddles: how can people enjoy food without compromising their health? I was not only loving my meals more than ever before but also feeling like I was so healthy I could walk on the moon.

Our launch was much more than another restaurant to me. It was the beginning of my second career and the opportunity to express a clear vision: that food could be healthy and delicious at the same time. We went all out with the opening. We hired my former publicist, the joyous Karine Bakhoum (who was now a Chodorow devotee), and invited all of the city's food elite. Within the first week, they would descend on our indoor and outdoor dining rooms: Alain Ducasse, Bobby Flay, Joe Bastianich, chefs, models, celebrities, and plenty of raw food fanatics as well. It seemed we were the hottest place in town for a moment, and soon enough, reservations were hard to come by. People were loving the heirloom tomato lasagna, beet ravioli with cashew cheese, and Thai lettuce wraps. And critics were nice—far nicer than expected.

Gael Greene, the critic who both launched my career in 1991 and memorialized its descent in 1999, was kind:

> I've been ignoring this nutty trendlet, hoping it would go away. And when Matthew Kenney started soaking nuts and sprouting grains, I wrote it off as a midlife crisis. But I've sat in Pure Food and Wine's magical garden, learned that rice distresses one's colon, and popped rice-free sushi into my

> mouth with chopsticks made of corn. To my amazement, I actually like the little rolls stuffed with pignoli and jícama. Indeed, our quartet of gourmands is beguiled by tomato tartare, the spicy Thai lettuce wraps, and a pineapple-cucumber gazpacho (anywhere else, it would be dessert). Soft corn tortillas with chili-spiced "beans" taste surprisingly Mexican. After zebra-tomato lasagna, hummus-slathered flatbread pizza topped with a savory salad, "creamy" golden-squash pasta with summer truffles, and dessert, I cancelled plans to stop for a burger on the way home. All around us, vegans are rejoicing: "I'm a vegetarian and kosher," says the perky twenty-something at the next table. And "My guy's a vegan, so we couldn't be happier."[8]

New York Magazine, *Time Out*, *Crains*—they all raved about us. Press was positive, and the critics, kindly, did not drag my previous crash-and-burn into their reviews about the new concept.

Frank Bruni, the *New York Times*' new food critic, was mixed in his opinion, but it seemed journalists were either too confused or too lazy to criticize us. Overall, we were happy with his opinion:

> Pure Food and Wine abides by vegan dietary restrictions and belongs to the raw food movement, which holds that conventional cooking with a usual intensity of heat amounts to a kind of nutritional apocalypse, laying waste to vital vitamins and turning important enzymes into gastronomic refugees. The restaurant sets a ceiling of 118 degrees.
>
> Pure Food has a serious pedigree and big ambitions. The moneyman behind it is Jeffrey Chodorow, a veteran of

> China Grill and Rocco's on 22nd Street. One of its chefs is Matthew Kenney, who turned heads, before he turned away from meat, at Matthew's on the Upper East Side. (The other chef is Sarma Melngailis.)
>
> They have taken over what used to be the restaurant Verbena, painted the walls a sexy shade of red, and planted fresh herbs along the perimeter of the back patio, a fantastic outdoor space for which many a restaurant would forever swear off veal.[9]

Like so many restaurants, Pure faced high staff turnover after opening, and while a new team was ushered in, a culture began to form. There was one minor problem: winter. As it cooled off and the gorgeous patio closed, we soon discovered that the place took on a different personality. Revenue dropped to almost nothing, and by December, when most restaurants were busy, we were losing $40,000 or more per month. Some nights, we saw fewer than twenty guests for the entire service. We closed for lunch. I could see where this was headed, right back into the brick wall I had just extricated myself from. I prepared for the worst, although we kept at it and somehow found the strength to keep trying. Chodorow asked us about adding raw fish to the menu and surely had thought about utilizing the space for another concept.

Working through the winter without a general manager or bookkeeper, we took on whatever responsibilities we could ourselves to keep costs down and ensure that the lights stayed on. There was anxiety every month as our numbers came in. It was frustrating to see Mario Batali's Spanish restaurant next door, Casa Mono, packed to the rafters on a nightly basis while we would see our last guest to the door at 9 p.m. Things were looking bleak.

And then, as if a veil was lifted, January brought an uptick in diners, perhaps influenced by the relatively consistent press, but more likely coming from return guests who intuitively knew this food would feel better than dining on pasta and bread and meat after the food-filled holidays. Little by little, business grew the old-fashioned way. By summer, when we opened the garden for our second season, the restaurant blossomed. It was filled nightly with an interesting crowd: a mix of health nuts, celebrities, models, locals from Gramercy Park, and a lot of regulars.

By our one-year mark, although we were used to seeing famous faces, nothing had really translated into growth for our aspiring health and wellness brand. This night, a server came to the kitchen looking to summon me to her table. The guest wanted to talk.

"I'm going to publish your next book," she said.

I'd heard of Judith Regan, the controversial publisher who formed Regan Books under the umbrella of News Corp and Rupert Murdoch. She was glowing and confident, just the type of person you want to deal with in publishing, which sometimes comes with endless delays and apathetic communication. I'd started with a cookbook agent, but I'd grown tired of the treatment and was going to negotiate this on my own.

The next week, Sarma and I were in Judith's office talking about our book deal, and we signed an agreement shortly after. *Raw Food, Real World* would document our journey into this new realm with the tagline: "Get the glow." We felt like our lives were glowing, inside and out, and we wanted to share that. The recipes and photographs were done mostly on site at Pure, and we did the writing in our spare time. The book focused largely on our personal experiences and, as a result, would contain a number of photos of my partner and I together: "the perfect raw food couple." It would inspire thousands to live this happy life.

The only problem was that while we may have been glowing in our business life, we weren't as a couple. At that point, I was quite familiar and happy with sleeping on the couch. Neither of us would admit that although we produced some great work together, that was where the connection ultimately began and ended. Our book came out in June and was launched with a huge garden party: paparazzi, celebrities, journalists. By the time the book was released with our picture on the cover, drinking champagne and sharing the glow together, we were not together at all.

Although I was finally settling into my new home, things were clearly not going to work out. Sarma and I were on completely different planets, and Chodorow, always one to show his strength against chefs, took her side. I was cornered. Chodorow called me and suggested I "take the juice bar" and give up the restaurant.

My earlier business failure had taught me many lessons, most notably, how important it is to get back up and, in some cases, how it's relatively easy to get back up. I didn't sweat it so much this time despite the fact that I was going to leave abruptly without compensation. I had my pride intact, was confident in the work I was passionate about, and wrote Pure off as a stepping stone to getting my life back in order.

GREEN JUICE

Green juice puts you at the top of your game—physically, mentally, and even emotionally. Fill your body with the purest nutrients available and you'll be rewarded. Take an entire head of kale, fennel, a touch of celery, a crisp fuji apple, lemon, ginger, a bunch of cilantro. Run it through the juicer and enjoy the liquid energy. You'll be ready for anything.

FIGHTER

You know you're doomed if you release a book with yourself on the cover, pretending to be romantic and bubbly with your "partner," despite the fact that you barely speak to one another. In hindsight, it was a foolish thing to do. Sarma wanted to keep our separation private, which I can only assume was to keep the peace with our publisher and other business endeavors we had in the works. This made sense on some level, since our personal life was nobody's business . . . until we decided to broadcast it with this soap opera of a book cover.

By the time the book was released in June 2005, I was a good six months out of my relationship with Sarma, and things at work seemed to be stable between us. I was dating someone new by then, a beautiful girl named Natasha, and did my best to keep that relationship far away from the business. We never met at the restaurant or anywhere near it; I just kept my personal life away from work. Then came the book release party, and with the invite list, Sarma seemed to have come full circle.

"Sarma invited me," Natasha assured me.

I suspected no good would come of it, but I stayed quiet.

The book party was a great event, attended by some big names, industry types, and paparazzi. Despite being a hot and sweaty New York night, the garden was buzzing. Petite versions of our signature dishes were passed out to the guests, along with organic libations, our signature sake mojito, and lots of bubbles. Raw food was about to swing for the fences.

Natasha sat in the corner with a friend, and later in the evening, after having a couple of vinos glasses myself, I may have sat pretty close to her as well. I left the event feeling great about things, and despite the oddball aspect of working with an ex, everything seemed to be looking up.

My apartment at that time had a bedroom window with a little marble ledge facing the beautiful steeple of Grace Church on Broadway and 10th Street. I had a chair in front of the window where I could sit and think. I was fond of those morning window meditations, and I was relatively comfortable in my chair on this particular day when I felt my cell phone ringing in my pocket; it was a number I didn't recognize.

"Matthew, this is Jared Paul Stern."

A call from Jared was never a good thing. He was one of Richard Johnson's gossip writers, searching for content for page six of the *New York Post*. Jared was a bit of a punk, a fedora-wearing semi-intellectual who would later get booted for trying to bribe a billionaire; but I was not a billionaire, so I was fair game. I knew nothing positive would come of speaking to him, but he'd nailed me on the phone, and there I was.

"So, you had a book party with your partner and brought your new girlfriend . . . "

He went on to explain, not verify, his version of the "facts." Nothing I could say would change his story; this so-called fact-checking call was a formality at best.

The bold headlines said something along the lines of "Raw Food Power Couple Splits."

I still believed all this drama would work itself out. After a year of hard work, the restaurant had become profitable, and our book was going to be a big success and had released to positive reviews. Chodorow agreed we should start looking at spaces in LA I had wanted to open a restaurant in Los Angeles for as long as I could remember, so this was a major breakthrough.

Still, I should have seen the writing on the wall. Each month, there was another excuse for why we wouldn't be paid on time. (It seemed that Chodorow quickly forgot that he'd scammed me out of $1.3 million with Commune, and his new version of events was that he was "helping" me by opening Pure Food and Wine.) Sarma was happy enough sucking up to him, but I wasn't. Between the two of them, I felt trapped. And I couldn't really focus on my bigger-picture goal of taking the restaurant to the next level and bringing this newfound cuisine to the world. I started to consider other options. I also realized I needed to hedge my bets a little to ensure I had an alternative plan should things at Pure not last forever.

Out of the ashes of the long-gone Bar Anise came a friendship with an affable guy named Raymond who'd kept the books for Selim. He'd gone on to work in a legitimate restaurant and had opened a nice but dumpy little place in the East Village. He was a well-meaning guy, and he wanted to do a good job, but his place lacked imagination and was simply behind the times.

Raymond invited me over and explained that he was tired.

"I've been running this place for ten years. I need a break, and you have good ideas. Why don't you take it over?"

It was just around the time that wine bars were starting to pop up in New York, and we felt we could do something cool and modern that would be a great fit for this space. I put together a most unusual partnership: my friend Russell, who built Pure, and an Irish subcontractor named Mickey (of course). Mickey delivered the $25,000 deposit to me in a brown paper bag, and I handed it to Raymond.

We spent a few weeks transitioning Raymond's tired little place into a dark and warm room with high communal tables, a small outdoor patio, and a glowing wood-burning oven in the dead center of the back wall. We called it Winebar, simple and to the point. I hired a talented young chef and let him do his thing; the cuisine wasn't what I was now focused on, and I was still busy with Pure. The place had a nice crowd, did well, and, although it was a small side project for me, would give me an exit door should I need one.

Back at the raw ranch, things were getting more and more dicey. Each afternoon, Sarma and I had a 4 p.m. meeting with the management staff, a strategy I employed to reduce the unfinished deliverables. Sarma never missed a meeting, except for one. The day that she was absent, it all became clear to me that while I was biding my time hoping things would work out, my partner and Chodorow had been colluding behind my back to take the business away from me. My brother is the one who woke me out of my denial.

"They are trying to get you out," he told me bluntly.

I had a hard time digesting this. I had designed the restaurant, essentially built it from scratch with Russell, and put together the team to run it without much help at all from either of them. I had treated Pure as my own child, finding savings in used materials to keep the costs down, recycling chairs and equipment, and forgoing all design and architecture expense. I'd recognized every critic and food writer, had given my blood, sweat, and tears to the project, and had begun a very successful program to teach classes in a new room we'd built in the back called "Pure Kitchen."

These courses were populated by a wonderful group of students, mostly female, who came from as far as Connecticut, Washington, and Pennsylvania. I was so inspired by teaching, and the classes were so consistently booked, I realized that this was a great opportunity. Teaching made me feel energized, and, especially as this food was so new, I was really charged each time I was able to share the new ideas and techniques we'd been learning. The revenue for the classes was also good, another reason we should have had a very peaceful partnership. We even took a sliver of a space to the side of the kitchen and opened a cute little juice bar called "Pure Juice and Takeaway," which was generating $2,000 to $3,000 a day. I was giving 110 percent to the company, and that made me vulnerable.

Chodorow still held the restaurant in his name; I was relying on him for living expenses. Sarma had formed our personal holding company, and we had no formal agreements there. I would soon be reprimanded by my attorney to the other side of earth and back for not having formal agreements in place. And yet, there is only so much an agreement can do to ward off ill intentions.

I stopped getting paid, and instead was getting cornered. One weekday afternoon, I realized I may never set foot in Pure again. I wasn't about to go to court to fight a bitter ex-girlfriend and a multimillionaire convicted felon—this battle would have to be won over time. As they say, success is the ultimate revenge, and all I wanted was to build my dream company, show the world what real food could be, and establish a solid business model while doing it.

The last argument Sarma and I had was on the edge of the back patio, and I made my position clear: "You can have the restaurant. You can claim it's your creation and play owner as long as you want. It may be one year, three years, or it might take ten, but the day will come when it is clear to the world who created this and where the passion really came from."

I left and never returned. That night, I changed my phone number and went to Winebar for a glass. I had a plan.

My biggest fear at the time was losing my platform to develop raw food ideas, teach more classes, and share this new way of looking at food with the rest of the world. I knew I wanted to incorporate the four components—education, hospitality, media, and products for takeaway—that I had found successful at Pure into whatever I did next and expand on them. I enjoyed holding classes, and I knew teaching was critical if this food revolution would ever reach more people. I loved producing books and hoped to eventually bring this cuisine to mainstream television. Of course, restaurants were now in my blood, and I believed—and still do—that the fast, casual aspect we'd produced at Pure Juice and Takeaway could eventually be fast food's solution to the unhealthy conundrum.

In one bold move, I put together financing to open a vegetarian restaurant, a chain of juice bars, and a publishing deal for two new books. The restaurant was on the Lower East Side. It required nearly $400,000 to purchase the lease and a lot more to renovate the place. It would be called Heirloom, and I had enlisted some of the Winebar partners and their friends, all rough and tough Irish contractors, to be my partners.

Somehow, I found the space, made a deal with the owner, and put the capital together less than thirty days after leaving Pure. Then I moved to Brooklyn, where I would oversee this new endeavor.

The media was kind once again. It didn't look good that I was leaving Pure, although we had done positive work and the restaurant was a success. Overall, the press positioned what I was going to do in a positive light as I put together a new company to hold these various projects called Organic Umbrella. I had visions for what this new company could be, perhaps a bit early on, but I knew a multi-faceted lifestyle brand was entirely possible, and it could influence lives across the globe.

JACKSON POLLOCK RAVIOLI

This edible art puts coconut flesh to an unusual use: blend the coconut well and spread the batter-like mixture onto a drying tray. Splatter the spread with the most vibrant vegetable juices—spinach, beet, yellow pepper—and don't worry about making a mess at all. Just let go. Dry the mixture on the tray for four hours, at which point the texture will resemble a wonton skin. Wrap about a cashew-herb puree and enjoy.

EXPANSIONIST

I had to buckle up for this ride. Moving to Dumbo in Brooklyn was quite the culture shock after living in Manhattan for eighteen years—it was cool and industrial—and the bike ride across the Brooklyn Bridge at midnight wasn't something I could see myself doing in the winter. Still, things were looking up.

All six new locations opened at essentially the same time: Heirloom on the Lower East Side, The Plant and Bluegreen in Brooklyn, and Nolita in Connecticut and on the Upper East Side. My close friend Lenny was my partner in Brooklyn and it was a good thing. The environment there was tougher than Manhattan, and we had a landlord who only responded to Lenny's brand of communication: no B.S. Lenny also made it fun. He could be as hard as nails over the little things, but whenever a real challenge came up, he took it in stride, even with humor. We had a blast and it nearly killed us. We produced our signature desserts and snacks at The Plant, commissary-style, and shipped them out to various locations daily. Raw food is hard enough, but when you add in packaging, transportation, rotation, marketing, and staffing, it becomes a whole different animal. I had a relatively comfortable life when the process was confined to one location at Pure, but this was pure madness.

Although Heirloom had been the biggest investment, my passion was The Plant. It embodied everything I believed in. It felt like an art gallery, a blank canvas for unbridled creativity and education, all housed in the modern, industrial aesthetic that inspired me. This was the most creative year of my life. I had been exiled to a warehouse in Brooklyn, but that wasn't about to stop me from expressing my vision for what raw food could become. On the contrary, I wanted to knock it out of the park, to kill it. And we did. This period set the tone for everything I would do with the rest of my career.

When you give it your all—just pour your passion into something—and if the work is good, it really doesn't matter where you do it or what the circumstances are. We were in a previously rundown open space next to a power plant, serving the most cutting-edge plant-based food in the world on communal tables with casual service, and photographers came out of the woodwork to see what was happening.

We started holding private dinners on Friday nights, and they were packed. These Friday night menus were wild, usually with simple titles. Guests loved "Contemporary," a meal inspired by my favorite great artists, including "Jackson Pollock Ravioli," "Rothko Terrine," and "Cubist Mushrooms" (a nod to Picasso). One of the most memorable meals was the Kubrick-inspired menu, a close second being "The Rolling Stones," and third, perhaps the *The Wizard of Oz* theme or the Willy Wonka menu. Not all the menus were based on celebrity, however. "Black and White" was pretty cool, with its tuxedo dumplings of young coconut and black sesame. These dinners were only once a week, so they gave us license to push the envelope, and the guests thoroughly enjoyed it. We generally poured a pretty generic white wine, something called Tisdale, but coconut water was the drink of choice.

The classes we held at The Plant were also a hit, taking raw food education to the next level. Some lasted all day on Saturday and Sunday, others were two- or three-hour weeknight events, and they were very well attended.

Meanwhile, our juice bars were operating without a lot of oversight from me, and there were several issues. Raw food is not something an attendant can throw together, so this model suffered, and our quality standards were far below those we aspired to.

We had so much going on, it was hard to do any of it well. A company that grows organically can put systems in place along the way, but our growth was just too much all at once. This was in part due to my ambition but mostly due to the fact that raw food was starting to gain some traction. People were realizing that they could enjoy food and health together. It just required artfully prepared food, not the brown globs that people associated with eating vegan. We had that part right—our food was glowing and full of life.

But my partners at Heirloom wanted profits immediately. The restaurant had a nice audience, but being vegetarian—versus raw, or even vegan—sent a mixed message. I had compromised what I believed in for what I felt would work in a certain location, and the result was food that lacked the crispness I'd grown to love. Ironically, our chef had also been my chef de cuisine at Pure. When I left Pure, I received emails from her, as well as a few other key employees, and I hired four of them.

No sooner did we have our doors open than I was slammed with a lawsuit by Chodorow and Sarma for "inducing [their] employees to leave Pure." In court, we encountered all kinds of drama and whining.

While I was the one who should have filed the action, instead I was defending myself. During a preliminary arbitration, the judge denied their claims and even suggested that the two colluders offer me a settlement for my role in Pure. They offered me $50,000 with a bunch of strings. My attorney told them what they could do with that offer, and we walked away with no strings and no money. Before the case could go to trial, Chodorow's attorney had an unexpected heart attack and died, and the thing seemed to just wilt on the vine. We never pursued them, and they never pursued us. Technically, I never forfeited any rights to Pure, but I'd let it go emotionally well before this drama ensued.

When Heirloom failed to hit a profit in ninety days, my partners started clamoring for meat. I could see where this was going. I should have learned that no business opportunity is worth being in an acrimonious partnership. I was outnumbered (again), and I was too tired to fight, so after a few grenades, we agreed to disagree, and I moved on in my own direction.

My partners at The Plant were also ready to close, but I know they were worried that I would resist pulling the plug. Normally, that would have been the case, but the timing wasn't right for this endeavor; it had happened too quickly, and it wasn't going to work. We agreed to let The Plant go and move on with our separate paths peacefully.

Around this time, I received yet another call from a "journalist" who pretended to be interested in a factual article about my trials and tribulations. I understand you're fair game when you are a public figure—the journalists might praise you, but they also have a right to rip you to shreds, so long as it's factual.

The article had a photo of me standing outside of The Plant, just before a Friday dinner service. They did a nice job catching me with a severe look on my face, an indication of stress that did not exist.

The article was titled "Into the Fire," and it started out:

> Matthew Kenney's restaurant career hasn't been short on drama—accolades appearing alongside gossip-page sniping, awards followed by closures. He is, in many eyes, New York's most profoundly enigmatic chef—a sometimes brilliant, resilient one whose story is filled with all the makings of a Hollywood movie: good looks, bad relationships, heartbreak, and deceit. And lawsuits, lots of lawsuits.[10]

I wasn't too upset by it, but I was annoyed that this mediocre writer had the power to attack me, and I had no recourse. I think he expected me to sue him for libel, but I shrugged it off and focused on my next chapter.

I had to let it go. After what I'd been through with my original company, then with Pure, and now this, I felt I'd hit a permanent wall. Physically, and even emotionally, I could keep going, keep doing what I believed in, but I needed to find a new way. I had to stop repeating the pattern of trying to rely on retail, brick-and-mortar business, especially in a city such as New York where rent was so expensive. (Our little 300-square-foot juice bar on Mott was over $6000 a month!)

I called my friend Rob, who had introduced me to the raw food world, and asked him to meet me for lunch. Rob was pretty direct with me, after hearing about my latest issues and reading the *Time Out* article.

"Matthew, I believe this dance with New York is over for you."

Rob had struggles on Wall Street years ago and went to Europe for some time, windsurfed in St. Barth's, and found his way back to New

York eventually. He liked to think he and I had similar paths. But I still had such conflicting emotions.

Everyone I spoke to agreed; I needed a break from New York to get some perspective. Friends have a tendency to support life-changing decisions; however, when you're forty-one years old, essentially penniless, and have a dream that you believe must be brought to life, it's not easy to go camping and take each day as it comes. I had a small income from a new consulting project in Midtown, FreeFoods, which would allow me to live modestly for a few months, plus my two-book deal, which I was hoping to salvage in light of the fact that it was based on The Plant. I just needed to decide where to go.

One friend suggested skiing in Austria. "You can ski all day, then 'après ski'—get blasted—and write all night. You'll have an incredible time."

Loved the idea. Couldn't afford it. More and more advice came in.

"Move to Paris. You should have been a writer all along."

"LA, baby, that's where it's at with your food."

I knew the LA suggestion was spot on, but I couldn't imagine starting at ground zero in LA. It was my end goal, but I did not want to arrive in Tinseltown without a pedigree. Two unwritten books and a consulting job for a deli wouldn't really qualify as much in the land of glam.

My close friend Amna suggested Montreal. Finally, the voice of reason from someone I could trust.

"It's beautiful, European, and still close to New York. Winter is freezing, but the people are wonderful. I have friends you can meet, and you'll love it."

My one-year lease in Brooklyn was up. I moved my belongings into storage, flew to Maine to see my parents, then bought a one-way ticket to Montreal. I didn't know a single person, and that's how I wanted it. After nineteen years in New York, it was an adjustment, but not one I minded at all.

This new city had everything I needed at that moment: great yoga, organic foods, cultural diversity, and I found a beautiful little loft for a reasonable price given that it was the off season. For most of the next several months, I had a pretty simple routine: write early in the morning, work on my consulting project, practice yoga daily at a wonderful studio called Moksha, and walk for hours each afternoon. And think. I hadn't stopped in years, and this was the first time in my adult life when I could reflect on my career and life—past, present, and future.

I actually took time to rest. I watched TV! The yoga transformed me, as it always has. The healthy plant-based meals I made—along with a few dinners a week at the local vegan café, Aux Vivres—rebuilt my body; and the sleep—what a foreign concept!—made me feel great.

Still, my rejuvenating stay in Montreal was short-lived. Although I was mostly off the radar—I wasn't on Facebook or any social media—I did receive an occasional inquiry about new projects. One was for a raw food café in Winter Park, Florida. The young man who contacted me, Joe Diaz, was a banker who was looking to do a juice franchise and somehow landed on my website. We agreed that I would consult on his opening and this would provide me with an entry back into the world I loved: raw food. We'd call it Café 118, meaning nothing would be heated above 118 degrees Fahrenheit.

We started working remotely just as spring set into Montreal. The crickets in the fields began chirping, the bitingly cold afternoons that became dark at 4:40 p.m. thawed a touch, and people were on the streets. Just as Montreal was waking up from its winter slumber, I saw those singing birds and optimistic faces as a sign that I was ready to re-enter the world. Not that Montreal is not a great world—I loved it and met some wonderful and beautiful people—but it wasn't my world. I had no future there. I was ready for Florida and the "big leagues" again.

KIMCHI DUMPLINGS

Chefs never know when a dish may become a classic, but we know the feeling when a new one comes together and all the pieces gel. Coconut is often a vehicle, a wrapper for innovative fillings. In fact, when bundled with the Korean favorite kimchi and napped with a white sesame foam, a product of whipped almond milk and a hint of toasted sesame oil, the dish takes on an ethereal elegance. Umami is possible here.

UNDERDOG

There is something romantic about any artist or craftsman languishing during a major career lull, though it's rarely possible for the artists themselves to enjoy it. Despite my success with Café 118, I would soon be heading back to Maine without much of a plan. Consulting with FreeFoods was still enough to cover my living expenses, but even on a good day, I was standing in the same place, getting older, and missing opportunities.

In one of those final days, Joe handed me a note with a message—a woman from Oklahoma City had called Café 118, asking to speak with me. I'd never been anywhere near Oklahoma and, frankly, wasn't even sure where it was. I didn't know if the call was from some type of collection agency or just another person with a recipe question.

"Hello, this is Matthew."

"Well, hi there, Matthew. My name is Dara Prentice, and my partner, Mandy, and I are big fans."

Dara had one of the loveliest voices I'd ever heard—deliberate and clear, making me feel immediately comfortable. She explained that she and her friend were opening a raw food restaurant and school in

Okahoma City, and they wanted to me to design their kitchen. I had hung a shingle, so to speak, on my website, noting that kitchen design was one of my services.

Dara forwarded me the business plan for the restaurant, 105degrees. She asked me to put my thoughts together.

My proposal for the kitchen design was quickly approved. I received a very generous fee that allowed me to really focus on the project in its entirety. Although I felt like my culinary and business creativity were still in exile, it still felt good to be a facilitator for others and their dreams. My biggest concern was the common sentiment that raw food in Oklahoma made very little sense. But I was intrigued by the clean, modern architecture of the location there and allowed myself to venture down memory lane while summoning up some inspiration.

A few years prior, while on book tour in Texas, I had an afternoon off during my stop in Fort Worth. The location felt about as rural and western as any city I'd seen outside of television, and I certainly did not expect that I could experience anything cutting-edge. I was accustomed to visiting galleries in New York every weekend around that time and was surprised to read about a beautiful, Japanese-designed modern art museum just outside of town. The Modern Museum of Fort Worth was stunning, surrounded by an enormous infinity pool.

I walked the museum for a couple hours and retired to the café, a very comfortable space enveloped in curved glass. With the experience of a single spectacular location, I was transported. That same spirit of creating energy where it was least expected inspired me to delve deeper into the Oklahoma project.

Dara and I were having regular conversations, and she asked me to become more involved.

She and Mandy offered me 10 percent interest in the business in exchange for my ongoing support to design the project and serve as the Executive Chef. I was delighted; I saw the project as a mostly blank canvas. Together, we agreed to build a full-service café and to create month-long courses in the academy, with weekends and evenings reserved for local classes. This project was well-funded, unlike the courses at Pure Food and Wine, and offered every opportunity to build a world-class facility. My goals for this project were nothing less than to build the most outstanding raw food establishment in the world.

I arranged a flight to Oklahoma City to meet in person. As the plane descended on the beautiful winter afternoon, I watched as we passed acre after acre of flat land and farms followed by some oil wells pumping the ground as we approached the airport. All that emptiness made me wonder where not only the food but also the guests would come from. The population in Oklahoma City was said to be a million, though one would have to cast a very wide net to come up with that number. I grabbed a cab to head downtown.

Downtown Oklahoma City, the location of one of our country's worst disasters, the bombing of the Federal Building in 1995, is clean, quaint, and very, very quiet. Nobody was on the street on this Saturday afternoon—not a soul. The hotel seemed quiet, too.

An hour later, Dara, just as elegant and charming as she had been on the phone, picked me up. We had a pleasant dinner at one of the city's better restaurants. It was fine, although the cuisine led me to believe that we may be a bit ahead of our time here. During my two-day visit, we went to the site, located among an expansive flotilla of partially finished black steel and glass buildings surrounded by red dirt. I could see what they were going for, though, and was excited by the similarity to my beloved Texas museum. I left OKC with unbridled excitement about this project.

Shortly after I signed on, Mandy withdrew from the project. Dara and I divided up the responsibilities: I would be handling operations from food to service to education, and she would oversee the business, legal, and financial affairs. Dara was one of the most meticulous people I've ever worked with; when she was on, there was nobody like her. We divided up Mandy's shares in the company and proceeded on with planning and development. Soon after, it hit me that I'd never operated a school before.

In the past, I'd always poured my energy into my own comfort zone, but over time, I have come to embrace the unknown. I believe my experience in Oklahoma should be credited for providing me with that initiative. We were really developing three businesses at once: a large restaurant, with a huge dining room, bar and patio; a retail shop; and an academy. I gave each of these projects intense focus.

This would be only the third time in my career where I had a completely raw space to develop the best layout for what I wanted to accomplish. I envisioned a completely transparent back of house and a dining room that relied on the activity around it rather than walls with art and other décor. Every detail of this restaurant—from the glass "box" retail store and gorgeous outdoor patio to the lavender Desiron chairs ordered custom from my contact in NYC—was refined and elegant.

Meredith Baird—the confident twenty-something who'd handed me her business card at one of our fancy dinners in Brooklyn—would serve as our Director of Special Projects. Meredith and I had seen each other a few times since that night and stayed in touch, but it wasn't until more recently that she emailed me inquiring about a possible position with my company. I was excited to have her join us, and our collective creative juices created something truly incredible.

You could feel the tangible buzz—as well as a bit of puzzlement—in the community about this project. The physical space was stunning, no doubt, but a kitchen without fryers and a refrigerator without meat were uncommon arrangements in these parts. Indeed, when our health inspector arrived—a wiry and ragged older man with a shiny tooth and a glint in his eye—he squinted at me as if I were an alien.

"We like our meat bloody here," he said. I took that as an indication that he may not be the first customer to line up outside.

Oklahoma City was landing dead last on some recent lists of America's most "fit" cities, and it had a mayor whose main initiative was to improve the city's health. It felt like we were in the right place at the right time.

While the new chef we hired was organized, experienced, and reliable, his food was not where I had hoped it would be by the time we opened, and I struggled with that. I had always been able to rely on teams who could not only uphold my vision, but expand upon it. That wasn't the case with this kitchen—the food was attractive, but mechanical. I hadn't had enough time working with this team yet, and our cuisine was too new to them. I wasn't pleased and knew I'd need to spend a bit of time assisting.

The Academy, on the other hand, appeared to be under control and was so rewarding. The students were perky, fresh-faced, and excited as we met them for orientation. I envisioned a school that would provide students with the skills required to bring raw food to the mainstream in a way the public could embrace. Education is empowerment in that it involves sharing and giving. It also happens to be a much more pleasant business to operate, with fewer variables than the diabolical restaurant scene.

On opening day, we were packed. The restaurant struggled under the crush of patrons, but we got through it. People seemed happy. It wasn't the most hyped opening I'd ever done, but it wasn't the lowest energy I'd experienced either. No doubt, there was not a raw food facility like this anywhere, and I wondered if there ever would be again. This train had left the station, and what a ride it would be.

THAI GREEN

Join the green smoothie movement. It's here to stay, and I love it. Chilled or frozen pineapple and mango work well with a little almond milk or coconut water, a touch of coconut butter, a big fistful of kale, perhaps a sliver of ginger, and a big mug. Drink it all.

EDUCATOR

In NYC, sometimes, it feels like it's all show. In Oklahoma, everything seemed much more real. Oklahoma has a rare style of hospitality and a casualness that put me at ease right away. Still, it was very different from where I'd grown up and spent my life, so I struggled to find my internal balance.

At the Academy, though, our diversity made it seem like we were in any major city. Our first class was made up of a half-dozen students from all over the United States. One was a very successful blogger from Georgia. She wrote about the course daily, which resulted in many inquiries about our programs. Being a start-up in the middle of America without a marketing plan wasn't easy, so the new leads were a saving grace.

This was my first time running a business that was not based primarily on a restaurant. The Academy occupied much less space and had far fewer employees, but as far as the financial model went, it was equally as important as the café. And, in terms of our big-picture goal to change the way that the world thinks about food, the Academy meant far more than one dining room could. If each of these students went on to spread the word about raw food in their own way—through teaching, writing, blogging, starting their own business, or even simply feeding their families better—it would be one step toward a healthier planet.

Although the curriculum had never been tested, there was much to share, and we loved every minute of it. It was important to me that our classes be entirely practical, meaning that students would be learning nearly everything by doing it themselves.

When I went to the French Culinary Institute, usually one student did the cooking while the rest of us watched. I didn't want that to be the case at my Academy. Also, at French Culinary, I had learned at a very gradual pace. My schooling had been a six-month course, and I felt that much of that time was unnecessary considering what I'd been taught. If we'd had more equipment and a different structure to the curriculum, it would have enabled much faster learning.

I knew a six-month course in Oklahoma would likely be both cost-prohibitive and time-prohibitive for out-of-area students—especially for those from overseas. We decide to run our Level I course, Fundamentals of Raw Cuisine, as a four-week course and offer an advanced course called Advanced Raw Techniques, initially as a three-month program.

We took some major hits in that first year in the Academy. I kept thinking back to French Culinary and how that business started up with a class of six people, just like we did. I saw how it had grown into an impressive powerhouse, changing the way chefs thought about food and creating a powerful brand along the way. And in that same spirit of change and discovery, I felt that we could offer even more.

During a business trip to New York shortly after we opened in Oklahoma, I passed by my Alma Mater in Soho. Walking down Crosby Street on a crisp autumn afternoon, I saw a group of students who happened to be out on their lunch break. Almost every one of them held a can of soda or a cigarette, or both. This made no sense to me. Even when I was in traditional school, I never would have considered putting those chemicals in my body. It destroys your palate and, of course, your body—and these are people training to feed others.

Meanwhile, our students in Oklahoma ate monster leafy green salads or big smoothies for lunch, or they simply enjoyed the food they'd made in class.

At some culinary schools, the walk-in box holds only a handful of non-organic, barely edible vegetables or the cheapest fish imaginable, and instructors explain that the purpose of the education is simply to learn the techniques. Fair enough, but technique is only one aspect to culinary artistry. I vowed to never let our Academy fall back on this crutch. All of the ingredients in our Academy are, have been, and always will be, of the highest quality possible. We use the best and most modern equipment, and the curriculum is based on our proprietary, up-to-date recipes. To this day, we continually update our curriculum with the most advanced recipes we can create.

Still, despite this commitment to quality, we didn't yet know our audience. The Level II class was simply too long; three additional months in Oklahoma for a student from far away was a challenge, and we did not have the faculty to properly engage students for this long. It was apparent right away that Level II, a major aspect of our business model, was not going to work. We moved quickly to address this and converted the class into another one-month course that would be much more approachable yet still offer the high-level skills we could not teach in Level I.

Faced with the constant challenge of trying to have the kitchen produce food at the level we aspired to, along with a barely groomed Academy team on the fence of burnout and fatigue, I was concerned about the sustainability of this concept. My initial plan was to be in Oklahoma for three months, build everything up to where it was running smoothly, and then head back to the East Coast to continue rebuilding my career while still making regular visits to Oklahoma. Instead, other than a few business trips, I didn't leave OKC for more than a year.

Fortunately, one student from our very first class, Megan, stayed on with us. She was someone who carried an unusually high sense of ownership for everything she did. It started before we even opened when she and Meredith put together our gorgeous little shop. Post-graduation, she joined the front of house, working on the floor as a server, behind the bar, and also spending some time in the kitchen, working pastry. Ultimately, Megan became the Academy Assistant, and that is when things began to change.

Even though Megan was fresh out of school herself, she made us realize that running our school with anyone other than graduates teaching would be impossible. That experience factor was critical to maintaining consistency. Being a chef is a very intense job, so it's natural that many chefs, later in their careers, want to teach. However, the harsh reality is that, sometimes, chefs decide to teach when they simply no longer enjoy their restaurant careers or when they've lost their passion. I vowed that this type of placement would never happen in our classrooms. To this day, we will hire someone who is fresh out of school, as young as twenty two years old, as long as they have the passion, a technical understanding of the skills, and an ability to inspire.

Shortly after opening the Academy, we hosted a highly publicized event called "Live and Learn," a two-day educational and entertaining program on a weekend in September. This brought raw food "celebrities" from New York, LA, Canada, and even the United Kingdom. The house was electric on the Friday when they all arrived; the dining areas were packed inside and out, full of that star power you'd imagine in a

New York opening. This was different—it was every bit as dynamic, but for a different reason. Our guests were glowing with health. The Raw Model, Anthony Anderson, was here to speak about his journey toward becoming a plant-based fashion and environmental icon, and the LA–based chef Ani Phyo came to demonstrate her popular and accessible style. We had the Raw Runner, Tim Van Orden, who was a master snowshoe racer; Karen Knowler, an educator from the UK; and Philip McCluskey, who had lost over one hundred pounds on his raw food diet. We also had the lovely Penni Shelton from Tulsa, who was really one of the leaders in the growing social movement around the plant-based world at that time.

The local community also supported us. We had a great event program, and we invited OKC public figures to host each night as our "Rawkstar" chefs. The first was a favorite local chef, Ryan Parrott. He was known for his Mexican cuisine, which we adapted to be raw. Other figures included Barry Switzer—the famous NFL and NCAA football coach—and OKC mayor Mick Cornett. We held a charity event for St. Anthony's Heart hospital (where I was honored as the first guest chef who wasn't a television food network chef) as well as a number of other high-profile events. We enjoyed a colorful cast of regulars and certainly made a mark, not only in the region, but also in the world.

Still, the reality was, after the dust settled, we were on an island—actually, an island off the coast of an island. Our space was in a new area called Classen Curve. Our landlord originally promised that all the spaces around us would be rented within four months of our opening, but a year later, we were still the only tenant who had opened in the gorgeous, enormous, empty, new retail development. It was dark at night; nobody could find us, and the retail food traffic we counted on was non-existent.

In year two, our Academy started to thrive, but the restaurant struggled. By this time, my vision for what a pure kitchen should be was pretty cohesive, and our space—with its white Carrera tables, polished concrete floors, soft lighting, and music everywhere—was modern and elegant. This impacted the food and the way people perceived it. We had built a raw food dream house; while Pure Food and Wine was cozy and warm, and the garden beautiful, 105degrees was a virgin—new materials never touched by cooked food and its accompanying grease and grime, no meat or fish, and it was all sustainably put together.

Despite this, it was hard to find a staff that was passionate about our cuisine. I found for the first time how nearly impossible it is to build a strong kitchen team from a group that had never experienced raw food and, even more importantly, who didn't live on it. While New York is loaded with vegan chefs and even mainstream chefs who have tried and enjoyed vegan cuisine, the members of Oklahoma's culinary brigade who could tell a good vegan dish from an average one—much less identify and prepare a cutting-edge, world-class, raw food revelation—could be counted on a couple fingers. Our food was quite attractive, respectable, and also respectably inconsistent. But I knew that without a stronger team around me, our mission was going nowhere. Our chefs were incredibly talented technicians; most could prepare the standard eater a meal that would blow their socks off. But it wasn't enough for us.

That isn't to say that we weren't successful on many levels. Even with a staff entirely new to raw foods, we went on to get some major recognition including being named by *Forbes* as one of the ten best new restaurants in America that year. In fact, we were getting major press across the board.

The biggest problem was that people were having a hard time warming to the idea of food that wasn't warm. Although we had a healthy group of loyal regulars, we were admittedly in the dead-center of the wrong state for vegan—much less raw—food. We were not bleeding too badly, but the entire venue was losing close to $100,000 a year. This is a lot of money, and yet, for a new and complex business, it was possible to inject enough to still operate.

Then, as if we didn't have enough problems, my partner and the original visionary of the project, Dara, pulled out. After about three months with minimal involvement, she emailed me, explaining that she would be stepping aside. In a way, a business in Oklahoma that I was solely responsible for was about as unlikely as any scenario I could have imagined just two years ago. I would have to figure out how to run it with limited resources, and I would be stuck spending the majority of my time on this project for at least the next year. At the same time, I had no choice. We referred to the operation as "The Little Engine That Could."

I was tired, though. I missed my time in Maine, was nowhere near my family or friends, and was in a climate I couldn't wrap my head around. Some friends urged me to consider going back to mainstream cooking, but this was my passion, and I couldn't imagine turning my back on it. Still, I questioned my business acumen at times. I wanted the entire world to eat this way and feel the benefits, but I also needed to survive. Well into my 40s, this wasn't a game for me.

For a while there, at least several months, I just chugged along and did my best, waiting for the right wave to flow into. Sometimes we can create our openings, and other times, we must watch for them. This was a watching moment.

THE GO-TO LUNCH

Everyone needs their own version of comfort food, but it doesn't need to be unhealthy. Think simple: a little steamed kale, avocado, a ferment —sauerkraut, perhaps—a couple sheets of nori, and you're set. Food without mood: no need to feel tired and heavy after lunch. Just energize and enjoy. Trust me, you'll crave it again.

SPEAKER

When someone calls you "rock star," you can take it a few different ways. Take it literally, and you're likely to crash and burn before you get off the ground. Alternatively, if you brush it off entirely, you're missing the wonderful fact that someone really believes in you—unless, of course, they're just pulling your leg.

For all his glossy, cringe-worthy commercialism, Jack Wilson certainly believed that I was a rock star. We've all heard the theory that everyone comes into our life for a reason. After seeing many of these reasons firsthand, I definitely buy into that, and Jack, for all his flaws, brought me into a new realm.

Just after taking full ownership of the Oklahoma location, I received an email from Jack asking if I had any graduates to recommend as a chef for the raw food restaurant he was opening in Greenwich. The discussions evolved into a partnership deal: I would provide consulting services and retain 25 percent of the profits. Jack promised to oversee the time-consuming task of negotiating deals, arranging appearances, and creating the overall strategy of my career and brand. He had a space on Greenwich Avenue—nothing big or fancy, but it was in a good location—and a goal to bring well-prepared raw food to his community. No question, I was tired and a bit worn down, but Jack put together a deal that gave me hope. I still believed that anything was possible, that we were doing revolutionary work and doing it better than anyone anywhere, so I was willing to explore any means of stepping up our game.

But first, Meredith and I were invited to a very special event, a cruise to Central America.

I didn't see Jack for the first two days of the cruise, so we did our best to entertain ourselves—playing basketball on the deck, reading, and finding spots on the ship to avoid the gluttonous behavior that surrounded us in every direction. We had to scrounge the various restaurants on the ship to find a few walnuts and oranges, pretty much the only thing we could eat that wasn't covered in some scary sauce or glaze. I'd learned long ago that most food on cruise ships starts off on the wrong foot, with ingredients that are frozen and often out of season. Then, to make matters worse, they are generally overcooked and heavily dressed, left in steam stables to stay warm, and eventually evolve into congealed, smelly, tasteless renditions of something that was perhaps food at one time. If I had forgotten how much my lifestyle had changed in the past few years since going plant-based, this trip was certainly a stark reminder.

Finally, on the third day, we met up with our elusive host.

"Hey, rock star," Jack beamed, ordering a bottle of Perrier Jouet in the middle of the afternoon.

There on the ship, he explained that he had "big things" in store for me. Jack's plan was to begin my "new career" in LA, which I'd been wanting all along anyway. He envisioned me as I had always seen myself: the person bringing together culinary art and wellness into one neatly-folded, attractive, delicious package. The way to do this, much like Martha Stewart had, was to not only operate at a higher level but to also develop a strong media presence. He claimed to have resources who could help us see that goal to fruition.

I was excited at the prospect of this partnership, but back on land, days passed and Jack was M.I.A. I'd forward him inquiries on a daily basis. A publisher wanted to discuss a book deal. Two or three days passed, and after reminding him, he had his assistant fire off a rude letter to them. Former colleagues from New York contacted me and asked if I would consult on a new project they were doing, offering a pretty large up-front fee and a piece of the business. Jack let them know that I was onto bigger things now and was going to be a rock star, essentially shutting the door in their face. I cringed every time he communicated with someone on my behalf. One by one, his arrogance turned off pretty much everyone I'd built relationships with and tore down the reputation of quick, cordial communication that I'd built for our company.

It's hard to imagine how I could have turned my life over to someone I barely knew, much less someone with such different tastes in everything but food. And yet, I did it, given the promise of progress and a better life. I agreed to hand control of not only my personal brand, but also my business, to Jack and his team. It did not matter that he had less restaurant experience than a twelve-year-old, or that his director of operations was a belligerent bully who reeked of cigarettes. The signs were there; I just didn't want to see them.

We changed the restaurant's name from 105degrees to "Matthew Kenney" and my likeness would appear everywhere—on the menus, on advertisements, and on the new website (www.kenneycuisine.com). Those menus were in the most obnoxious font (a dark gothic print on light green paper—think Irish Pub meets the Munsters) and my blurry black-and-white photo was emblazoned on the front of it. Jack set me up with Jerry, a $10,000-a-day photographer in LA who shot and edited my new photos, Photoshopped to the max with a big, toothy white smile blasting off the page wherever it was posted.

"Come join me, and change the world," was the slogan on the home page of our new website. All the beautiful photos were gone; the sleek and elegant design was history, replaced by a parody of the worst branding that The Food Network could muster. This guy simply had horrible taste. When you combine a complete lack of aesthetic sense with an alpha male, trouble abounds.

Jack wanted me to pounce on every table in the restaurant and tell them my story about changing the world one bite at a time. I always had to be "on," even if I bumped into a long-lost friend on the street. Cameras followed me everywhere, but the clips went nowhere. I was really so beaten up by the ups and downs of my career, the struggles in Oklahoma, and the fact that my vision just wasn't enough to create a sustainable business or a sustainable life for myself, that I was ready to try anything. Trying is one thing, but believing is another.

About a month into the Jack regime, my staff was ready to commit mutiny; our numbers—despite Jack's "marketing," coupons, and shtick—were flat, and Oklahoma continued to bleed. Tension was high. Although Jack promised to invest whatever it took and claimed that "failure was not an option," he whined every time the business needed a nickel.

Around this time, we received an email from a former prosecutor named Ken who was organizing a TEDx event in Oklahoma. (TED is a nonprofit organization that holds events to spread ideas by bringing together movers and shakers who give short but inspiring speeches. Originally it was an acronym for a focus on technology, entertainment, and design, but now TEDx events cover any range of topics.) Ken asked whether I'd be available to speak at the conference. As a big fan of TED Talks, I was both nervous and excited. I was still slightly shy about speaking in front of our students and would forever carry memories of when, as president of student council, I was unable to speak in front of my five friends without stuttering a dozen *uh*s.

After a series of meetings and discussions, we agreed that I would speak at TEDxOKC. Jack took control and poured more energy into this presentation than I'd ever seen him expend. The preparation was exhaustive. We had numerous conversations each week where he pumped me up about my duty to deliver a message that would change the world one bite at a time. I took speech lessons in New York City, days of being coached and taped and taught how to look my audience in the eye, about intonation, about confidence. I watched dozens of other speakers and tried to find my message, and I studied the script I was provided by Jack and some mystery team behind him. I took lessons from a ballerina who taught me how to walk properly and how to carry myself, and pored over the Powerpoint file that Jack's team created for me to use as an outline for my talk. TED Talks are eighteen minutes long, eighteen minutes of standing in a spotlight in front of two hundred people and other speakers who expect you to blow their minds with your brilliant orating skills and your earth-shattering message.

By the day of the conference, I'd spent countless nights memorizing my speech, practicing it to myself, on tape, to Jack, and even to an imaginary audience. Still, I didn't feel ready. I stayed up most of the night before, looking over my index cards, pacing, sweating, and losing faith that I had much to offer this inspiring audience.

My talk was titled, "Are You Feeding Your Body or Are You Feeding Disease?" It would touch upon topics that most in the audience could relate to: obesity, heart disease, diabetes, fast food, and cancer. It would also delve into sex and bowel movements, both of which I promised would be more fulfilling if one simply adopted a raw food, plant-based diet. The message was over-the-top, accentuated by images of smashed-up cars, highlighting the fact that obesity kills far more people than car accidents, and an entertaining exposé of the thirty-six ingredients found in McDonald's "healthy" oatmeal. It was overly dramatic and a bit tacky, and the style and packaging of the message had very little to do with me, but my talk would rise to become one of the top ten most popular talks on TED.com and would stay there for quite some time.

Everything I said on that podium was sincere, even if it was delivered in a wonky package. It was time to push some buttons, to not be shy about why I was doing what I was doing. I did believe that the world would be a better place if we adopted a plant-based lifestyle. I was embarrassed by the packaging of this message, but it was delivered in a spirit I supported with all my heart.

After the conference, I received numerous emails and calls from people who were inspired by my message, some asking for help. This was a major turning point as I finally realized that putting out beautiful food was not enough. I needed to share my experience and my beliefs in a much more direct manner. In turn, I could, in fact, change lives. As a society, we are so misguided; how can it be that we exist in a place where food in schools, hospitals, airplanes, homes, and restaurants actually kills us and contributes to disease? Natural food tastes incredible, and it can be delivered without compromise while still making us feel better than we ever have.

I realized that my mission was much more than serving good raw food, and that I should use every means possible to convey the meaning behind my mission. I was inspired by it. Nothing felt quite like empowering others to improve their lives.

Back at the restaurant, though, we were having a hard time realizing that mission. Business was pretty stagnant, and I was having difficulty collecting my stipend from Jack. Our bank accounts in Oklahoma were often negative, and I'd been stripped of my purpose and authority; I was barely hanging on. Then, a week later, I woke early one morning to an email from Jack.

Jack was clearly in over his head; he was not the fat money cat he (and we) thought he was and likely just realized that his so-called magic wasn't going to change much in Oklahoma. I could have told him that if he had wanted to listen.

Having been on the precipice a few times in my career, I had learned to enjoy the power that gets bundled up on a monumental decision. This was a poker game—Jack was threatening to shut down Oklahoma and liquidate it, an option he could essentially exercise if he so chose. I was weak, had no money once again, and was at his mercy, so all I could do was call his bluff.

In the end, I told him we had four options:

1. We work together on a new plan that makes sense.
2. I put together a plan that will require less funding and will resume the original point position that I had with OKC.
3. We determine a way to undo our agreements, allowing you to recoup your monies over time while handing me a stable business that I have enough of a runway to work with.
4. You take it over without me and buy my interest, and I'm free to grow as I wish.

Ultimately, we agreed on the third option, except the company he handed me was anything but stable. I took back a business that was $14,000 in the red with payroll looming and additional debts still outstanding. After I griped a bit about the condition of things, Jack wired me $7,000 as a "personal token." Everyone said I was "crazy for taking the place back," but I'd heard that before, and I got to work quickly.

I immediately signed a new book deal, a television deal, a consulting deal, and revived pretty much every deal that had stalled and died under Jack's regime. I was so elated to have that dead weight off my shoulders; I was moving about like a young lion, feeling nimble and free and energized.

Shortly after achieving freedom, I received a tentative invitation to appear at another TEDx conference, this one a much higher-profile event in Santa Barbara, CA. They had seen my first talk, which had done well, and while they liked the message, they weren't impressed with the delivery. The organizers, Mark Sylvester and Kymberlee Weil, were passionate, intelligent individuals who were not willing to cut any corners at all, and it showed from the first conversation. I had to try out to be formally invited, and this required three or four conversations about how I would structure my talk, what the subject matter would be, and what would be inspiring about it.

After some rigorous phone interviews, I had my arms around how to deliver this talk, and they seemed comfortable and excited. I had to dig deep to my core to really refine my message. The theme of the event helped: "The Spark Within" was an exploration into the inspiration that drives innovative ideas. Interestingly, it would be held on November 11, 2011: 11/11/11. This date was powerful!

After weeks of reflection and scribbling on my giant sketchpad at the drafting table that served as my desk, it was clear that I ardently wanted my platform to focus on changing the supplier of food, not the consumer.

Chefs are largely the culprits behind the obesity epidemic—they are the "drug dealers" in my mind. My previous TED talk, using Jack's approach, was to scare people into changing their habits. But that never works. People are pleasure seekers; we want to consume beautiful things that taste good, end of story. I had believed for some time that 300-pound chefs serving mammoth, Flintstone-sized portions, chefs doing drugs, or chefs who simply succeeded while ignoring the impact of food on the consumer—and themselves—were the real issue at hand, and that things in the food industry had gone way off track.

Late one evening, sipping a glass of wine, I wrote a phrase on my sketchpad:

Crafting the Future of Food

This is what I wanted my talk to be titled. It summed up my core belief, and I was also sure the organizers would like it. My previous TED Talk had been shared and posted numerous times, and everyone seemed to love it . . . except me. I knew it wasn't my true voice, with all the speech coaching and ballet lessons glossing my performance of Jack's version of the message. But this one would be all me.

A friend from many years ago put me in touch with a design group who specialized in presentations, and we created a Powerpoint deck that I thought was ten times better than Jack's tacky images. I spent weeks writing every minute of my talk and worked tirelessly to learn it.

Two days before the event, I flew to LA and stopped for a night in Beverly Hills, spending the entire evening in my hotel working on the presentation. A car arrived to take me to Santa Barbara the day before the event, and I spent the entire beautiful drive up the coast reading my note cards. I cued up for my rehearsal shortly after arriving and came on stage with my notes, all of sudden feeling completely lost. I could not remember anything and had been immediately transformed from a CEO to a crumpled mess on a stage. My palms were sweating. I looked down at my notes, read a sentence, paused . . . read another. No eye contact.

"Matthew, are you okay?" Kymberlee said, meaning, *This is garbage.* And I knew it was. "You can't use notes here."

But I'd used notes at the last talk! I thought everyone used notes at TED. This was crazy! But here I was, the night before, giving my speech, and Kymberlee was clear: no teleprompter, no notes. I was dead.

That rehearsal was one of the biggest disasters of my career, a complete flop that made an impression on nobody. If I didn't have a message, I could have accepted that, but my heart was exploding with passion for a lifestyle I believed we would all benefit from and love.

It was one of the most grueling nights of my life: I got perhaps one hour of sleep, drank a couple glasses of wine, and picked at a room service salad. I paced the hotel room, sweating, took a couple showers to stay warm and awake, and took copious notes all evening, scribbling, cramming, memorizing, speaking out loud.

By morning, I was completely lost. I'd changed so much of my talk in the night that I had no clue what I was going to do. Somehow, I managed to clean myself up; the hot shower cleansed my bloodshot eyes, and my crisp white shirt gave me a good clean look. I arrived to hear the first speaker, a brilliant doctor speaking about the magic of posture, and the audience was mesmerized by him.

I had about ninety minutes until my talk, and I was completely unprepared, so I went out to a back parking lot, surrounded by thick trees and stones, and started trying to deliver my speech to the air. I am not an air guitar guy or a shower singer, but thirty minutes later, I was reaching so deep into my belly for this message that I was literally yelling into the sky, expressing my passion to the wind and the trees. It was finally coming out, but it had no organization at all. What I remember most from this day is screaming at myself: "You are screwed! I'm so screwed!!"

I was at the point that I knew going on that stage would be speaking suicide and I could either opt out or look like a complete fool.

I've been blessed with great friends and mentors my entire life, and one that I'd just gotten to know better was Tom Dillon, a talented corporate hospitality guy from New York. Tom was calling my mobile, but I wasn't in the mood to chat. I didn't need words of encouragement; I needed my notes!

"How's it going?" he asked in his ever-casual voice. "I'm going to drive up and hear your talk if I can."

I wasn't in the mood for small talk.

"They told me last night we can't have notes, and I planned the entire talk around my cue notes," I tried to explain. He wasn't having it.

"But you know the stuff, right? You'll be fine."

I explained to him that an eighteen-minute speech was twenty pages or so of text. Sure, I could ramble, but TED was about precision; it was the heat-seeking missile of talks. After ten minutes of this banter, he finally got it. I was not prepared for this, and I was on edge.

"Well then, just get up there and let it rip!"

Those were the best words I'd ever heard.

It began to sprinkle outside, and soon it was raining. I was under a thick tree, screaming my talk to the crows and sparrows, trying to get the anxiety out of my belly as the clock was winding down. Somehow, it all began to gel. Finally, I went back inside—a little wet, a little nervous, and more than a little determined.

Next in line, I watched the ticking timer on the speaker before me, a seasoned pro, as I waited in the shadows. And then, I heard my introduction.

I walked out, took a deep breath . . . and let it rip.

My talk wasn't perfect. I was nervous. I forgot a few key points, and I was far from the best speaker in the house, but the point was made.

Plant-based food, in the right hands, could change the world, and I was committed to ensuring that would happen.

Kymberlee gave me a hug—one of the most important hugs of my life—as I exited stage left. Later that evening, I boarded the plane, dried sweat coating my entire body as I exhaled and contemplated what had just happened.

"We are crafting the future of food," I told myself. "Hold on to that."

SCOTT W'S CAULIFLOWER

Live and die by the seasons; embrace the beauty of the colorful, vibrant produce that each season has to offer. Combine purple and ivory cauliflower—thinly sheered and diced—crunchy smoked walnuts, earthy walnut cream, the aromatic spice of harissa. Try as you might, it would be impossible not to plate this dish in style.

ANGELENO

Although I was not physically tied to Oklahoma, our company's image was identified with it. We had built a great reputation, but we'd also faced many challenges. The market was clearly not ideal; products for raw food were hard to come by, and it was not easy to find strong team members who would relocate. Put simply, Oklahoma City is not a convenient or appealing location to someone from the East or West Coast, despite "being in the middle."

California, on the other hand, is ground zero for health and wellness and particularly for innovative, plant-based cuisine. While most cities' vegetarian restaurants are low-key affairs on side streets, you'll be just as likely to find paparazzi and a celebrity clientele in the West Coast establishments, where guests are aware and active in environmental and animal rights causes. I'd wanted to be there for years, but the market was always one that was rumored to be unfriendly to outsiders, challenging, expensive, and fickle.

I'd been to LA numerous times, usually staying in West Hollywood or Beverly Hills. Coming from New York, it felt eerily quiet on the sidewalks—despite the gorgeous weather—which was something I thought I could never get used to. It wasn't until a visit to Santa Monica, when I took a bike ride down to Venice Beach and over to the hottest street in Venice, Abbot Kinney Boulevard, that I found what I thought must be the most desirable place on the planet.

This street had the artsy feel of Soho without the commerce, without any trace of Starbucks or Jamba Juice, and yet all the fashion and good food one could imagine. The streets were crowded but not uncomfortably so, and bikers were everywhere, on cruisers and fixed gears, mingling with the pedestrians, their dogs, and their coolness. I was immediately attracted to the "West Side" and in particular the Venice Beach area. Santa Monica had the most impressive farmer's market I had ever seen, and the outdoor culture, expanse of the sea, and nearly perpetual sunshine was a dream. But going from Oklahoma City to LA without a true West Coast base was no small task.

After nearly a year of searching, we were finally able to sign a lease on the top floor of a high-end, indoor/outdoor mall in Santa Monica. I was shown the space by a close friend who had previously opened a couple restaurants on that property, and although it was awkward, I felt it could work for us and our new restaurant, M.A.K.E. Despite the competition, I believed the new Academy would be able to carry us, even if the restaurant took some time to get its legs. It wasn't quite right yet, but I was optimistic.

It was only after signing the lease in Santa Monica that I began to realize how little infrastructure we actually had. Matthew Kenney Cuisine was a brand without a foundation, a product without an operating system, and the lack of support created a few challenges working in this new environment. Most things, as usual, went wrong. Construction was delayed, staff was difficult to put together, and I became concerned about our ability to execute. I fell back on doing what seemed like the only viable option: focus on building a team, and a good one.

Meredith and I were the only long-term members of the company at this point, although I was fortunate around this time to welcome Scott Winegard to our team. Scott and I had worked together years before at Pure Food and Wine. He was a gentle soul with a roaring fire of creativity below the surface, a rock-musician-turned-chef with some pretty intense tattoos and a love for vegetables. Scott had recently staged at Noma, the world's number one restaurant in Copenhagen, and after months of conversations, he joined us as Director of Culinary Operations. Scott was just getting started but not fully immersed in it all yet. We hired an original manager from Pure Food and Wine, and Juliana Sobral, a friend of mine, joined us as the Matthew Kenney Operations Coordinator, a position that would finally put some order to my various business plans. The way I saw it, we had one summer to get our ducks in a row.

I started with what I considered the heart of our cuisine: innovation. We took possession of a gorgeous 1874 brick building in Maine, and we were only using the ground floor as an office, so we decide to convert that to a test kitchen. It would be called Plantlab, and despite all the work to get Santa Monica built, we found time and resources to develop a gorgeous laboratory that would serve as our creative hub in a building we owned. Plantlab was outfitted with everything a raw chef could dream of: a Pacojet thermal immersion circulator, an ultrasonic homogenizer, smoking guns, an anti-griddle—you name it. The lab was an expanse of gorgeous walnut cabinetry, raw brick archways, granite, and shiny equipment. This space would symbolize our commitment to consistent and persistent creativity.

On the West Coast, we first launched the Academy: Matthew Kenney Culinary. We originally planned to operate schools in both California and Oklahoma, but it quickly became apparent that students, given the choice, would prefer the beach, so we made the hard decision to close the Oklahoma location. This was the end of an era, but the move was necessary. Aside from being slightly larger than the Oklahoma location, and with a new system that allowed students to bypass washing utensils and equipment, the CA Academy felt very similar to Oklahoma, loaded with Carrera marble, stainless steel, and glass; it was gorgeous.

M.A.K.E. was another story. Set inside a mall that the developers must have seen as the next Ferry Terminal Market, M.A.K.E. was surrounded by a hodgepodge of random vendors without a clear focus. Across the hall from us was Nice Cream, an ice cream stand, and a pretty standard but well-run bistro called The Curious Palate. There was a chocolate shop, a coffee bar, and a cheese shop—a few nice options, but the area wasn't very cohesive or well-branded.

Still, things came together better than we expected. Of course, we had the regular hiccups. Our wine license was a complete disaster that almost derailed everything until we called upon every contact in our Rolodex, and the health department made us feel like we were selling heroin to school children, despite the fact that we were peddling vegetables to people who needed them.

Like Pure Food and Wine, this restaurant was built on a very modest budget. We were coming from a respected but low-profile place in the heartland, and one that had barely made a profit most years, so funds were scarce. Our landlord provided us with a substantial TIA (tenant improvement allowance), which would cover most of our construction costs, although we'd still need to purchase all the furniture, fixtures, and equipment, which would be a substantial cost.

I tried to put this project together from a distance, but our lack of organization became painfully obvious about four weeks prior to opening when we realized that we still had not been able to make any major decisions. This is where alignment started to work. In a single day, we hired our woodworker to produce tables, benches, and planters, and our interior designer to do the academy tables, marble counters, and a number of other touches for us. Three weeks later, the place was ready to serve.

While all this pre-opening activity was unfolding, I was settling down into my new California lifestyle. I fell in love with the blooming red morning sky, early runs on the beach, and visits to the infamous Gold's Gym, where I'd be doing pulldowns next to Lou Ferrigno, the Incredible Hulk himself. Although this new life did not have the mystery and magic of my entrée into New York City, it offered me a different type of inspiration—simply being in the right place at the right time. I wouldn't grow as I had and learn what I had in those early days in New York, but timing and alignment creates life-changing synergy. And that's how it felt.

I bought a bright yellow, Polish fixed-gear bike and started riding it everywhere. The ability to bike to all of my appointments—work, the market, or to dinner—felt like such freedom. Everyone whines about the traffic in LA, but unless you're trying to navigate jugglers, freaks, and tourists on Venice Beach, you'll never have traffic on a bicycle.

At M.A.K.E., we were fortunate enough to be surrounded by a passionate team of managers, servers, bartenders, and kitchen staff. When you're serving food you love for the right reasons—not simply to fill bellies or satisfy a gourmand's desires—you draw a different type of person to your team, a more dedicated friend, employee, and ambassador for what you do. Our space may have been awkward, but Scott's food took all that we had done in the past years to the next level. We hosted a few nights of friends and family, gave some press tours, and we were off to the races.

California and the world responded more favorably than I could have ever imagined.

Besha Rodell, the respected critic from *LA Weekly*, reviewed us less than ninety days after our opening. Her review was titled, “M.A.K.E. LIKES IT RAW: And You Might, Too, When You Try Matthew Kenney’s Santa Monica Restaurant.”

She is no pushover, and this was no puff piece; our cuisine was given many compliments along with some constructive criticism. Her closing paragraph acknowledged the flavor and elegance of our work while suggesting we also add a few more basic dishes and noting concern about our location:

> M.A.K.E. is about showcasing the tricks and discoveries Matthew Kenney has come up with, in presenting the raw-food recipes with the biggest wow factor. As a novelty, or a treat that’s far healthier than much of what’s out there in the dining world, M.A.K.E. displays the inventive and often delicious potential of raw food. The question now is whether the odd location can support that effort.[11]

The big name in food criticism in LA, and in the United States as a whole, is J. Gold, as Jonathan Gold is known. He is the first journalist to ever be awarded a Pulitzer Prize for food criticism and has earned his stripes, not only from endless exploration into thousands of meals and restaurants, but also from carefully studying the lineage of the cuisine we enjoy today. Gold’s reviews tend to celebrate animal meals, particularly hearty, rich preparations of pork, beef, and lamb. In his review, we expected to be slaughtered, no pun intended. If he ripped us to pieces, life would be hard. We did not have the great location I had enjoyed in New York at Pure or the insulation from the outside world we had in Oklahoma. A scathing review in the *LA Times* would decimate our restaurant traffic and also instantly remove a lot of the credibility we had carefully built in our Academy over the past few years.

In fact, one of the reviews he published just before ours was of Mario Batali's offshoot of his well-known Mozza. It was a meat-centric storefront called Chi Spacca:

> But you have come to Chi Spacca for the meat—if not for the steak, then for the spice-rubbed lamb shoulder chops, or the stuffed, braised veal breast, or for the bony, intense braised lamb neck that concentrates all the flavor of the animal into a few taut mouthfuls. There is a grilled *segreto*, a lean fillet of pork prized from a section of the belly, much more commonly seen in fancy Spanish restaurants than in Italian ones, and a "tomahawk" pork chop, a monumental rib cross-section that actually dwarfs the fiorentina, rubbed with fennel pollen and grilled slowly until it becomes what great spareribs might be like if Alabama bordered on Umbria.[12]

I could not fathom how any critic could appreciate this smorgasbord of animals and still enjoy a meal at M.A.K.E., but I also realized that no major critic in the United States had ever given a full review to a raw food restaurant. The first three paragraphs were essentially warnings to potential diners, including:

"Unless you are unusually attractive, M.A.K.E. is probably not a good place to drag a cranky carnivore on a date."

And then he started to absorb it a bit. He began by giving me a bit of credibility:

"Still, I knew that Kenney came from a different place than the hustlers and dietary evangelists usually associated with the raw-food edge of cuisine."

> In 2013, a lot of the techniques of Kenney's raw cooking are also found in modernist kitchens: Coi, Manresa, and Alinea, etc., where dehydrators, Vitamixes, and silicon sheets are as commonly used as pots and pans. M.A.K.E., with its attached cooking school and juice bar, is scarcely out of the mainstream. Meaty slabs of king oyster mushrooms with asparagus and sea beans; paper-thin slices of cauliflower jutting like fins from a disk of a kind of harissa-enriched vegetable couscous with walnuts; or a spray of thinly sliced carrots erupting from a base of cumin-scented nut butter are dishes you might see in any modernist restaurant in the world . . .
>
> Will three or four meals be enough to sway a hardened raw-foods cynic? Of course not, any more than a trip to Mastro's Steakhouse will persuade a vegan to switch sides. But it may be enough to make him take a second look.[13]

Thank you, J. Gold!

While Gold may never join the raw food movement, he understood that we were operating at the same high level as other avant garde restaurants, and that was good enough for us.

Later, the reviews would be even better than that. *Food and Wine Magazine* named our Culinary Academy one of the "Best New Cooking Schools in the World," and another noted journalist stated that our cuisine was "a revelation."[14] We had managed to hold our own in the most discerning city there is, and we were still standing.

COCONUT CARROT SOUP WITH SESAME AND CILANTRO

Rethink it all with raw food. A carrot's deepest flavor comes from the juice, so juice it for a liquid recipe. Thicken the juice with fleshy young coconut and half an avocado; spice it up with a good kick of cayenne, a touch of sesame oil, some sesame seeds, and a ton of fresh cilantro. Blend and chill or drink the rich soup at room temperature.

ENTREPRENEUR

A few months prior to opening M.A.K.E., my friend Tom and I were snared in traffic on the LA freeway in a tacky rented silver Corvette convertible and were doing our best to get to Anaheim for my dinner at Expo West, the nation's best and largest natural food show. He was driving; I was reading the parade of emails hitting my inbox. One of them caught my suspicious eye. The name didn't seem to be real, and the content was surreal.

It was a single sentence asking if I had a chef available to work for a well-known couple, one of the world's best athletes, a star quarterback, and his equally accomplished supermodel wife. Celebrity means very little to me, but my mission to take plant-based food mainstream relies on it. Nothing can spread the word faster than when a public figure publically endorses your product or work. I was excited by this, although I feared it might be a prank. Still, I made the call. Tom was now blazing down the highway, going about eighty, and the wind was pulling at my ears, so I had to duck down under the dashboard a bit to hear what the athlete's representative had to say.

"They're looking for a private chef and like the food you did at Pure Food and Wine. I'm talking to a few people."

I could tell he was used to having people kiss his tail, something I don't like to do, but I wanted this gig. I had been planning to launch a private chef placement service for years now but hadn't found the time or the in-roads to clients. This particular client would not only launch the placement business, but we'd be starting at the top. Still, from his tone of voice, I was one of many, and he just seemed to be fishing. I discussed our company's attributes at length, which seemed to impress him very little. We finally got to the point, and he explained that his clients would need a tasting before making any decisions.

"When?" I asked.

"They are in LA now. Tomorrow is the best day. They are at their new home in Brentwood."

I was in a Corvette, with no tools, and staying in a hotel. I had no assistants and essentially nothing to go on other than what I knew from publicly available information. I was scheduled to fly back to Oklahoma the next morning, but his client would only be on the West Coast for a short time, and I couldn't pass up this opportunity.

"Tomorrow is good. Can you email me location and time details?" I always err on the side of "going for it," but I wasn't quite sure how to pull this one off. Regardless, I knew this gig was important to our brand and an amazing opportunity for expanding the awareness of raw food in general, so I started dialing. I called up a colleague I'd never met, except through email, who had published some raw books.

"I know it's last minute, but I was wondering if you'd be interested in working an event with me tomorrow . . . "

She got back to me and said she'd do it. The next call was to a graduate of our academy whom I'd never met, but I knew he lived in LA. He was up for it! They both offered help with some of the more obscure ingredients we'd need—cacao powder and so forth—and some basic equipment I didn't expect this client's new home to have on hand.

I arrived at my hotel just after midnight and was due at the client's house at 3 p.m.; we would serve the tasting menu at 6 p.m., so that left us three hours to prep. This was intense. I felt like I was back on the line doing pre-theater at La Caravelle; my upper chest and neck filled with the brand of adrenaline that only a kitchen rush can bring.

I had a good idea of what I wanted to make: all the classics, nothing too risky, but everything had to be gorgeous. My initial thought was:

Shiitake and Avocado Vegetable Maki Rolls
Coconut Carrot Soup with Sesame and Cilantro
Heirloom Tomato Lasagna
Cacao Pudding

These were not our most advanced dishes, but with shopping on the fly and no car, working with a team I'd never met face to face, and only three hours of prep, I couldn't imagine anything more elaborate.

This would turn out to be one of the moments in which I'd fall in love with LA. My team members were spot on—just brilliant. They understood the food so perfectly, I was able to focus on my dishes while they prepped theirs. While we were organizing, our hosts stopped in and chatted—though I've never been one to be mesmerized by celebrity, the wattage of this power couple was undeniable. Public figures with a deep caring for health, wellness, and the environment are very special people. I really wanted this to work out as it would be a big stepping stone for our services business.

The meal flowed without a hitch, and my team and I were invited to come and talk to the potential clients. Given that we were all well into our 30s and 40s and in wonderful physical and mental condition, it was apparent that we were among the growing population who believed in wellness through what we put on the dining table—this was a turning point in my mind. I arrived back at the hotel after 10 p.m., higher than a kite about how things went. I was nearly certain this would be our first private chef client, and I was right.

The famous couple called us to make the arrangements the very next day, and we were in. If you are ever fortunate enough to start at the top, don't complain—it makes life much easier. Not only did this opportunity launch our new company, Pure Chefs Worldwide, but this client would also go on to recommend us to another high-profile client who then recommended us to more than a half-dozen others in a very short time span.

On one occasion we had a backstage tasting for one of hip hop's most notorious stars. Pulling our car right into the stadium, we were directed into a parking spot next to what I knew had to be the artist's wheels. It looked like Batman's SUV—a seemingly bulletproof, tinted out, supercharged matte black powerhouse machine. I'm not a car guy, particularly this type of car, but the thing was so hot it felt like we were sitting next to a lion about to pounce on its prey. It was impressive.

For all the hype about celebrity, most times I encounter a lot of handlers, spend a lot of time dealing with people who don't really know what you're about, and spend way too much time in cold, anonymous staging rooms. This one was no different, a concoction of cheap white materials intended to create the vibe of a cheap '80s nightclub. I was expecting the most obnoxious reception, given what I'd read, but this person seemed sincere in his intentions to incorporate raw plant foods into his lifestyle, particularly while on tour.

We presented a beautiful tasting, and he loved the food! I was expecting a booming voice, but instead, he was just a bit louder than a mouse:

"This is the best raw food I've ever had. Thank you, thank you. It took so much work to prepare all this, I want to share it."

It felt great, and I had new faith in the artist. Then again, shortly thereafter, his wife handed him a plate of ribs, which he proceeded to pick at. But it was a start.

It was clearer than ever to me that our brand would be about much more than education and hospitality. In order to fully change the way people eat and think about food, we needed to facilitate the process on every level: in the home, in the public arena, through products and media, and through all other possible networks. I was pumped up about our timing and the progress we had made.

Despite all the successes, though, in 2012, my work life was fraught with landmines and missiles and surprises—so many obstacles, in fact, that despite my health regimen, clean diet, and exercise, I still clenched my jaw at night. And around this time, I began forming a habit I'd wanted to avoid: living a high-stress life, having to be on at all times, and becoming a fanatical entrepreneur, obsessed with details, progress, and doing whatever was necessary to bring our vision to life. It wasn't about money or fame or anything other than a powerful belief in the need to build a world-class company based on plants.

I began to transition away from direct involvement with the menus and food as I saw Scott blossoming as a chef/artist. Meredith had already replaced me as the driver behind the book recipes and food styling in our cookbooks, and now Scott was taking my place as the creative force in the restaurants. I recognized that many culinary brands lost their edge as they grew, as the creative founder becomes more and more diluted when trying to balance brand growth and stay on top of trends and new ideas. I wasn't going to attempt the impossible. Acknowledging my limitations was a very liberating achievement, and I was comfortable knowing that our cuisine would not only remain consistent under Scott's guidance, but it would also evolve beyond its current state. Many people asked me if I "missed the kitchen." In reality, I reconnected with the kitchen; these small delegations allowed me to cook at home again, a habit I still try to enjoy several days a week.

In the new Academy, our student population continued to diversify to the point where a given class of fifteen students might be from a dozen different countries. I considered this our single greatest strength as a company. Our mission was to change the way the world thinks about food, and while I couldn't imagine reaching millions through our restaurants—after all, raw food isn't fast food, and I knew my mission in life was not to create RawDonalds—I did see our students as the real connectors to the outside world on a larger scale.

There was a lot of buzz about online education. Crazy Jack had suggested setting up a camera in the classroom and selling it as online education. His thought was in the right place, but the mechanics of what he suggested would have been a disaster. Typical classrooms may feel energetic to those immersed in the lessons, but to a viewer on a computer, the pace can feel incredibly mundane and dull. I knew we needed a different approach if we were going to break into online education.

My thought was that online education should not be seen as a compromise to being on site; it should have its own qualities that would surpass what could be offered on site. Sure, instructors could not taste students' work, but the reality is, the rest was not only possible but compelling in a new and unique way.

I envisioned the online academy functioning just like a classroom. The classroom starts the day with instructor lectures or demos, so the online platform would be the same, taught through beautifully edited videos and audio clips. I drew a map of how this would work. We would use the same twenty-day format, the same recipes (with some adjustments for geographical ingredient limitations), and there would be a number of cool features: live chat with instructors and lessons that were shot from three camera angles and in many cases planned out even better than on-site courses, with more consistency.

Working online was an opportunity to brand every step of the course and to reach thousands of students anywhere at any time. I envisioned the platform as having four components: (1) structured education, (2) a subscription portal for viewing the most recent recipes or entertainment we created, such as a foraging trip, (3) e-commerce to enable students around the world to access the specialized equipment, and (4) a community hub, which would bring together all of our alumni, current students, and team.

I've never been especially adept with the use of technology; digital watches have stopped working on my wrist, and my history with mobile phones had been littered with odd malfunctions. I couldn't use a navigation system to save my life and struggle to turn on a television in hotel rooms. But we all drive cars, and some of us even race them without fully understanding the mechanics; we do many things well without comprehending what the foundation is all about. My feelings about online education are the same. I don't care what code is required to build our dream; I care about the dream itself and specifically about doing it differently, better, and in a more innovative way than the competition.

This turned out to be one of my smoothest business launches ever, and we ran a beta test at the end of the year and launched successfully in January 2013 with a full class of students from all over the world. Online education could grow as far and wide as our imagination could take us, but my goal was to become the go-to online platform for the plant-based lifestyle. I had a clear vision for this online space, which would grow into dozens of impeccably produced courses ranging from culinary nutrition to biodynamic gardening—all things involved in growing a plant-based world.

Within that forum, I imagined a community that would bring together our on-site and online alumni and students with our team and even others from outside our circle. This nucleus could be a big part of the growing movement toward a new cuisine. I knew that if we could move all of this activity online, the students and alumni could manage it themselves, and if we offered them compelling resources to stay active, it could become a living, breathing interactive experience.

It inspired goose bumps to see real-time action taking place from all points of the planet, all built around our on-site education. We'd come so far in four years; I was humbled and grateful. You hear so much about tech launches being fraught with crashes and crises, but we really had none of that. The website did go down a couple times those first few days, and there were pages of modifications we quickly discovered that our web team had trouble handling, but the first edition of the Academy was solid.

Although I would have loved to pause and take a breath for a moment after the online release, we had many projects still in the works. *Plant Food*, our next book, was due in a few months, and a new restaurant in Miami seemed to be on track to open before summer. Miami would be our biggest project to date, a 4,400-square-foot gorgeous facility—just a dream of a project—that included a restaurant and garden designed by the famed Rene Rodriguez, along with an Academy similar to the one in Santa Monica, a glassed-in juicing room, and an infinity pool on the patio.

We would need to adjust our cuisine a bit for the Miami location; LA was not New York, and Miami was not LA. Miami was a bit faster at night, polished, and fun. The food would need to be colorful, bold, spicy, sweet, and vibrant. Our partner, Karla Dascal, was a creative and talented socialite who ran a very successful event business and was super connected to Miami's scene. We could not ask for a better partner. Still, there was a ton of work to be done.

As I sketched out our current business model, an exciting and challenging task, it became clear that I'd built a machine that was not the least bit on automatic; it required some serious elbow grease. I was physically a bit tired, but mentally I was fired up, coaxing the body to catch up to the mind.

MIDNIGHT SOBA

Room service and the Tokyo skyline. A glass of chilled sake and a box of soba—cool, but not cold—nutty and refreshing: a meal best eaten alone, quietly, in contemplation.

SURVIVOR

When you hear others talk about struggling to manage growth, it's easy to shrug it off as being an easy problem to have. The reality is, in those early days of 2013, I was feeling serious pressure. While my stress historically had been related to challenges that were hard to overcome, I now had such a passion for our brand that I could not bear the thought of not living up to our potential. Not only was I convinced that our company would set a new standard for plant-based businesses, but it also held the potential to become a standard-bearer for the best brands, a company devoted to education, social responsibility, creativity, and art and built upon a solid business model. Still, it was overwhelming to manage the growth, and my stress was mounting.

The workload and obligations I had were so tremendous that I woke up before sunrise every day, my jaw like a vice grip, feeling like a two-ton tractor was parked on top of my chest.

During this challenging time, I met the self-help author and guru William Whitecloud. He and his wife were dining at M.A.K.E. toward the end of the lunch hour, and I noticed he kept looking at me with a sparkle in his eye. I thought they must have been raw foodies who had one of my books and finally walked over to greet them.

"You must be the owner, eh?" he said in the all-too-familiar Australian accent. "I can tell by lookin' at you, and told my wife you must be. You have that look about you."

This visit was fleeting, but the next day, our manager handed me two books that William Whitecloud had authored and left for me. The first was titled *The Magician's Way: What It Really Takes to Find Your Treasure.*

Sometimes all we need is a little flashlight to guide us, and other times we need to be picked up and carried. I started reading *The Magician's Way* that evening and got into it before my trip to Tokyo, where I'd teach a week of private cooking classes. William's book, and the subtle attention he had given me, helped clarify my focus on results. I started to realize—not in a mystical or even spiritual way, but in a pragmatic, practical way—that the keys to reaching our dreams were to do what we loved and to believe in reaching our targets. I had a clear vision for where the brand was going, for what we would be, but I often allowed my internal battles to detract from the brightness of that vision.

This revitalized clarity could not have come at a better time. Our challenges were only beginning, and I needed tools to navigate through them.

Touching down in Tokyo, Juliana and I had a full day to rest and organize before teaching five days of classes to about ten private students. We checked into the beautiful rooms at The Peninsula Tokyo, and for a moment, looking at the beautiful Japanese skyline, everything seemed to be flowing. Within two days, though, it would all unravel.

Our landlords in Oklahoma were giving us serious pressure to reopen the restaurant, and it looked as though it would cost nearly $200,000. Sales at M.A.K.E. had flattened quite a bit, and the costs of building our online academy seemed to mushroom overnight.

This is the point where many people would conclude that they'd had enough, that life is too short, that sort of thing. I never entertained that thought. Things were tough, certainly, but our path was crystal clear to me. The business model made perfect sense; it attracted the best and brightest, both as consumers and employees, and our brand was solid. But I had spent too much time focusing on the product and not enough on the marketing, financing, and strategy. It was clear I was in for another rough patch, and I wasn't sure how to get through it.

We'd planned this visit to Tokyo for months, a tireless effort by numerous members of our team, our gracious host, and a lovely graduate who lived there. Japan is a culinary destination for every major chef, so I was extremely excited to be sharing our food with an audience both discerning and sophisticated. Our first evening was easy, a reception to greet us, which was attended by a wonderfully enthusiastic audience. We were tired, but this was uplifting, and we looked forward to the next day when we'd begin our course.

Waking up to work when traveling this far was tough, but the new sights and architecture on our drive to the space on the outskirts of town were novel and inspiring. We wound our way through a maze of streets, ending up in a remote little neighborhood about forty minutes away. In true Japanese fashion, the space was tiny, well-appointed, and efficient. However, we realized very soon that the "classroom" was, in fact, nothing more than a very low dining room table covered in plastic to protect the beautiful wood and densely populated with cutting boards, knives, and tools.

Most of the ingredients were still M.I.A.—no avocados, no herbs, no coconut. I looked around the room at the dozen or so eager faces, all smiling and anticipating that I would show them some raw food magic. I looked at the translator, who was waiting for me to begin imparting wisdom to this group. And finally, I looked at Juliana, who gave me a slight glare that said, "What's the holdup?"

"I can't work here." The words escaped my mouth, unbidden. "This is B.S., Juliana; I can't do this."

Juliana stays cool for the most part and even shrugs me off on occasion, but I could tell she knew this was a mess, and although her lips began to move, she shifted back and forth uncomfortably. Neither of us knew how we could possibly convey our work in this format. It's not about comfort or convenience; I would serve a meal in an alleyway if I felt the quality of our work would come through. I was worried that we would look like amateurs and leave our guests with an underwhelming experience.

I talked and tried to fill our translator with brilliant rhetoric that would buy time for avocados to miraculously appear, and they eventually did. This day never found its flow, but the students were good-natured, eager, curious, and polite. I was a grump and was trying to balance these lopsided working conditions with the incessant barrage of emails and text messages coming from the U.S. By day's end, when we hopped in the little black taxi to head back to the hotel, I was ready for a sake. We'd planned to head out to dinner, but both of us were pretty beat, and instead, we each had cold soba in our rooms and did our best to sleep.

Day two was a repeat, and on day three, despite some escalating issues in the States, we made reservations at one of the city's most well-known Shojin restaurants, the 2-star Daigo.

Just before dinner, I decided to log on to our bank activity to see what was going on. It was still business hours in the U.S. I have no idea why I did this, but something instinctual drew me to my laptop.

I looked at a few of our accounts; we had them linked for easier viewing.

$-999,999.999

$-999,999.999

They were all the same, one penny from being a million dollars negative! This was crazy! My mind ran through some possible explanations. Maybe something was going on with the banking system in the U.S., or maybe just at our bank, or maybe it was a computer glitch. I grabbed a credit card from a different bank, just in case, and headed off to dinner. A couple of sakes would be in order, but this wasn't a problem that a cocktail could fix, and I knew it.

Daigo is the type of restaurant that Japan is revered for, unforgiving in its goal toward hospitality and excellence. As our cab pulled up, a man no more than 4'5" wearing a kimono and a beaming smile held out his arm and led us to an elevator. Once in it, he made use of every moment on the ride up to the second floor to wink, nod, and laugh at the fact he came up to Juliana's waist. (She's 5'10" in flats.) This took the edge off the ceremonial meal we were about to have in a good and everlasting way.

We proceeded to enjoy a dozen or so beautifully presented, mostly delicious, and perfectly served courses of vegan cuisine in our own private chamber. It was one of my life's best dining experiences, and yet the thought of our cash flow problem weighed on my mind the entire time. We settled our bill and headed back to reality—Juliana apparently to sleep and me to my laptop.

$-999,999.999

$-999,999.999

The numbers hadn't changed. Assuming this wasn't a computer glitch, I hit Google for answers. Apparently, banks can randomly close accounts if they decide to, and this was the default computer reading to prevent any activity whatsoever. I called our banker. It was 2 a.m. in Tokyo.

He was kind, but honest. "I don't know what to tell you. I called the powers that be, and they feel that accounts are just too low and risky, so we're shutting them down. I'm sorry. You can wait five days to see what else hits, and we'll send you a check for anything that is positive at that time."

We had payroll two days later for about seventy-five people and no funds to work with. This was a blackout moment.

I didn't sleep the rest of the week. We worked and taught all day in the little room with the little table, and I'd lie awake all night, rising every thirty minutes or so to communicate with my CFO to figure out how to cover all these expenses. It was really a mess, and I know he was ready to fold.

The class was a great success, but as we prepared to fly back to Los Angeles, we were tired, weary, and stressed. I hadn't been ill in at least three years, but both Juliana and I had severe chills and aches on the plane ride. As soon as I arrived home, I went straight to my bathtub to warm up despite the fact it was still morning and sunny in Venice, CA.

We struggled for a couple months, but then a few things shifted. Enrollments picked up, as they always seemed to at the right time, and we placed a couple more private chefs—receiving substantial fees for the placements and bringing in some revenue to build up our new bank accounts and cover our overhead. I woke up at 5 a.m. each morning and worked downstairs in the dark, nursing my clenched jaw, and—through a combination of exercise, green juice, and perseverance—found my way into the light on a daily basis.

One of our Santa Barbara–based clients looking for a private chef came into M.A.K.E. one evening for a tasting by a potential chef. We held these in the Academy, and I made sure to be on site to meet the client as well as to offer support to the chef, who was a recent graduate. The tasting seemed to go well, and the client casually asked if we needed help in the form of an investment. I am humble by nature but also reserved, so I tried to leave the door open without appearing needy. I knew we had a company that could change the world, and people were starting to see it, but I also felt insecure about the position we were in.

A month later, we had secured funding that would completely eliminate our short-term financial concerns and agreed to give up a relatively small amount of the company. All those months of pain and agony, week after week struggling to meet payroll and keep our staff happy while I was sweating incessantly all night long—it just vanished for a moment, and I felt as if I had wings. But more than that, I was motivated. I was so pumped that others believed in what we were building as much as I did, and this is what now woke me up at 5 a.m. I was ready to fight this battle once again, this time with new fire in my belly.

PINEAPPLE GUACAMOLE

The avocadoes should be ripe, but not too ripe, and crushed with chopped green chili, a hint of lime, cilantro, a handful of cool, fresh pineapple, and sea salt. Your chips must be crisp. Guac is delicious with salsa, but even better with a hit of nutty chocolate mole and a cashew sour cream.

CAPITALIST

For the first time since imagining what this world could be like with the right cuisine taking hold, I was actually able to work toward our goals without severe financial pressure. This really opened up my heart and mind to the long-term picture. It's great to live in the moment, but when you're living to deal with the ongoing crises, it's not healthy.

This was a major turning point for me and the company. None of this is about money. Financial stability simply provides freedom. I am so connected to the vision of our company that it would be impossible to separate my personal life from my business. Some say that may not be healthy, but I believe in whole health, and if I'm pretending that the cause I devote 70 percent of my waking hours to is not connected to me personally, I'm deluding myself.

When I met David, our new client, he was kind and forthright. "It's really annoying when wealthy people are cheap," he said. "We want to help. We believe in what you're doing, and we want to see you succeed."

This would be the first of several conversations I would have in 2013, all with highly accomplished, brilliant people whose visions were aligned with ours. It was an interesting year as so many doors began to open, we could not possibly walk through them all. Still, it was fun trying.

One such opportunity presented itself close to home, in Maine. With all the time I'd spent growing the company over the last few years, I hadn't been spending a lot of time in Maine, but when I was there, I always looked forward to dining at The Lost Kitchen, a restaurant across the street from my parents' home. It was in an absolutely stunning flat-iron-shaped former bank building which was constructed in the 1870s. The Lost Kitchen was run by an eccentric-looking, artsy couple, and their presence really gave the town the sense that it was something special.

This year, I arrived in the late of winter, looking forward to several dinners at The Lost Kitchen's bar with my book in hand. This time, though, the restaurant was dark. I was devastated. The Lost Kitchen had been was one of the highlights of my time in Maine. Although it wasn't entirely a plant-based menu, there were many options, so it was disappointing that the place was now gone for good.

I do my best to build a life around quality ingredients, great food, fresh air, and the ability to stay fit and exercise. In this small town of Belfast, we had the States' largest co-op: 100 percent organic and filled with virtually anything that most Whole Foods stores could offer—even more, in some instances, given their commitment to supporting local producers.

This organic life was supported by local businesses and restaurants. There was an organic juice bar under construction, a project being developed by a young local entrepreneur that our company funded, and an absolutely incredible town landmark called Chase's Daily. Chase's, as it was called, was operated by a family who owned a farm ten miles from town. In the summer, they sold the most attractive produce that could be found anywhere, bundled with twine and presented in metal buckets and wooden crates, and all the prices were noted on a piece of shingle: "Beets, $2 a bunch." It's a magical place. The Lost Kitchen had rounded things out and given the town a foodie vibe that inspired creativity for me and our company.

Plantlab had been born in Maine as a means of bottling that creativity, and while Los Angeles was our business hub, the Maine coast fulfilled our goal of committing to innovation. I had seen so many companies, especially chef-driven businesses, that stopped evolving once the growth began. Regardless of how many restaurants we opened or schools we founded, without constant evolution, we would not achieve our goals. Raw food and plant-based food was still far from becoming mainstream, and it would have been completely naïve to believe we could create a shift in the market based on where we were or even where we would be in a couple years. Maine gave us the platform and the pressure to keep pushing, to reinvent, and to grow with each season.

In addition to these creative outlets, Maine had served as a hub for nearly everything we had created in the past five years. Our books had been written and photographed there, we had developed our menus for various restaurants there, we had built our online school and even filmed initial courses there, and our plan was to build the heart of our brand there. So when I got a phone call from one of the previous owners of The Lost Kitchen that spring, I knew just how to respond.

"Matthew, I'm not sure you know, but . . . "

The man went on to explain with a lot of emotion that things hadn't worked out between him and his wife and he was likely going to be in possession of the restaurant. He wanted to know if I had any thoughts about how he could proceed.

I pretty much set my schedule to the side and focused the next eight weeks on transforming the charming building into The Gothic. As soon as the town started hearing of my involvement, the rumors began that we would be a raw food restaurant as if that was not a good thing. That said, I intuitively knew that this restaurant could not go vegan overnight.

We launched as a beautiful space featuring local produce, seafood, and land animals. Our menu layout said it all: land, sea, soil. We devoted equal space to each of the three categories, demonstrating equally our ability to support the region's preferences but also giving a full billing to our plant-based inclinations.

The Lost Kitchen had been far more game-, butter-, and fat-heavy, so our cleaner approach, sans fries and with much less meat, made some locals with big appetites a bit resentful that our food was "fussy." This is always a challenge when teaching people how to balance flavor and health. Many people equate food that is light with food that is fussy; I maintain that if food is heavy, it's unappealing. We worked all summer to find a balance, and finally, we did. We seemed to have a commercial success on our hands. It wasn't perfect, and it never is, but the reviews were pretty solid, the place looked gorgeous, and the food was stunning and mostly well received. Still, I faced pressure from our core audience and one of our financial partners about the inclusion of meat. I, too, was torn, since I couldn't eat half the menu.

David, now one of our investors, made his position clear: "Matthew, perhaps it is my fault for not being clear, but we expect you to know that we do not feel comfortable funding a business that serves dead animals."

I buckled a bit because I knew he was right, and yet I was in a conundrum. I needed to find a way to grow our business and still balance our philosophy.

Meanwhile, we were finally set to re-open in Oklahoma after being closed for nearly six months. Our Director of Operations had overseen an extensive renovation that cost nearly $250,000 and had pulled together a relatively high-powered team of management. The new restaurant would serve Mexican cuisine, so we called it Tamazul, the name of a painting of a frog done by one of Mexico's greatest living artists, Francisco Toledo.

I was concerned about Tamazul's launch. All of my time had gone into converting the Maine location back into The Gothic, ensuring that it would open smoothly and be in line with our company's philosophy. With all I had going on, my time was limited, and I trusted our team in the heartland to build on our philosophy and, although not vegetarian, to open a restaurant that held a number of our company's core values. Unfortunately, there were some troubling signs.

Put simply, Tamazul lacked business smarts. My great friend and former business partner Boyd has said it best: "Matt, all business is the same. There's operations, marketing, and finance. Don't forget it." This restaurant had operations, at least functionally, but the product was questionable. I thought the guacamole, a staple in a Mexican restaurant, was terrible. There was little attention to budget, and the marketing was non-existent. We were essentially 0-for-3.

In the most inverted way possible, success was the worst thing that could have happened here—and it did. When Tamazul opened, it was packed out of the gate, bringing in numbers that were three or four times what the raw food place had done. The reviews were mediocre at best, though, and complaints were rampant. By this point, I had seen this movie dozens of times: the place opens, it's a hit, management believes it's due to their brilliance, overconfidence permeates the operation, and guests don't matter . . . until there are no guests. As Gael Green of *New York Magazine* so aptly predicted of my uber-hot Commune in NYC many years earlier:

> But then comes that apple strudel. And Matthew out of the kitchen looking dazed and weary. Let's hope he's wooing his lunch crowd because nocturnal birds have no pity, and when they catch a whiff of the next super-hyped water hole, all they will leave behind are the dregs of their Cosmopolitans and a few bent straws.[15]

Sales for the first two months were booming. The food continued to get pummeled by the diner reviews, marketing was still non-existent, and, most troubling, we had become a meat-centric kitchen. At this point, I was cautiously optimistic that Tamazul would just be one of those mediocre restaurants that makes a healthy profit; I'd keep it on our balance sheet, but not on our website. We were not remotely identified with the place, so this was my only hope. We peaked about two months in on a Saturday night when the restaurant did nearly $8,000 in revenue, a big number in OKC, but after that, the numbers began to fall.

Shortly thereafter, my director informed me that we needed to make a chef change. Despite the volume, he explained that the back of house was not being run professionally and there were many questionable things happening. Frustrated, I suggested my ex-girlfriend Liz's brother-in-law for the job.

Things were about to get interesting.

PUMPKIN IN ALMOND OIL

On the eve of a major storm, it's dry and cold with biting winds. Inside, there's soft light, a warm room, chefs in the pristine open kitchen, and hot almond oil over tender pumpkin, likely prepared en sous vide. *Keep it simple. Match the environment.*

LEADER

A group of young, passionate professionals on a plant-based mission, we were seated around the massive, white lacquer table in the all-white room. It was our first leadership team gathering in the history of Matthew Kenney Cuisine Global, and here we were at 9 a.m., underneath the soon-to-be-bustling Apple store in Santa Monica, in the briefing room. I looked around at the healthy glow of eight familiar faces, all gathered to lay out our action plan to grow our brand into a lifestyle company that would not only facilitate a massive shift in the culinary world but also mark the founding of a superior brand, one that contributed to the world's education, to the lives of its employees, and to the livelihood of many.

It was bittersweet. Gone were the days when I would sit with coffee or a glass of wine, pondering my next move and making hasty decisions—some brilliant, others that I would quickly pretend never happened. This group was serious, a team of leaders who were here, not just for a job, but to bring their passion to the table and to create a future for the company and for themselves. I felt a tremendous responsibility to them, to our investors, and to everyone, really—students, guests, and the thousands who had supported us. This was, all of a sudden, very serious business.

I looked around the room and tried to put myself in their shoes.

James Bartolomei was an intelligent litigator with movie-star looks who had moved with his lovely wife, Suzanne, from New York. I learned from past experience (ahem, Pure Food and Wine) that it was imperative to have a seasoned attorney on our team to avoid pitfalls related to unsigned documents and other landmines that appear when aggressively growing a business. Despite a background in legal warfare, James was a diplomatic and truly good guy with a compassionate heart. In addition to guiding our legal decisions, he would spearhead new business development, negotiating contracts and new deals.

Megan Massoth had, of course, joined us many years ago and was now Megan Dunn. She'd moved to Oklahoma to attend our Academy and ended up being our Director of Education, meeting her husband in OKC, as well. Megan hadn't yet moved to LA, but she was planning to and seemed to take each phase of our growth in stride. She is an old soul in a young body, and sometimes I feel that she can see exactly where this is all going with a clarity that escapes the rest of us.

Don Fields was our new CFO, stepping into the shoes of his predecessor who vanished into thin air when called out on some sloppy work. Don was the straightest shooter of the bunch, right out of Compton, and had been with some large operators, so our quick growth didn't intimidate him at all. I was always told that in order to build a true business, you need a great financial person by your side, and I felt good going into battle with Don.

Meredith, of course, had also seen this all evolve from a dog-and-pony show to a true business model. Her first month with the company was spent wrapping and carrying heavy copies of *Entertaining in the Raw* to the post office and then testing recipes in a grungy kitchen on the Upper East Side. In a way, she had grown up with the company and took this all very seriously, as it was tied to her own evolution.

Another old soul in a young woman's body, Juliana Sobral had a discerning nature about her that kept me out of harm's way and also brought a quiet, intelligent perspective to everything that we did. While some people may thrive independently, Juliana is the type of person every team needs—the voice of reason, the one who cuts through the fluff and makes the right moves. Juliana was adamant from day one about streamlining my role and recognized the dysfunction that would ensue if we didn't do that.

Our Director of Culinary Operations, Scott Winegard, brought the artistic edge to this team. His appointment was proof to me that we'd come full circle. I'd seen far too many companies that build up a group of corporate guys and girls without the creative voice having a say in the brand. This company would be different—I was committed to never stopping the innovation, always riding on the cutting edge, and actually letting the tail wag the dog. I refused to let the status quo into our operations, and Scott would never let that happen. His work in the past year had already taken our cuisine to the next level, bringing a sense of whimsy, lightness, and airiness to a food style that often feels overthought and overwrought.

We had specifically chosen Apple to host our orientation because of the programs they offered for business communications and as a nod to the innovation of the Apple brand in general. I knew we were about to embark on a path with no return, and once we made that commitment, nothing short of fire in the belly of every person in a leadership role would allow us to reach our potential.

Once we passed around comments and listened to our Apple hosts, Juliana and I laid out the two-day agenda, and we all headed to the private room at the Viceroy Hotel, a room with yellow banquettes, a shag gray carpet, and an overall mod-squad vibe.

We were all set up with Powerpoint, notepads, healthy snacks, and an intense agenda. I scheduled a full, intense day and named it "Ascension." We discussed why our company exists, our core beliefs, what we do, our strategic advantages, and what was important at that moment. The purpose of the gathering was outlining our primary goals and developing an action plan for the next year.

After the first day, we all had a dinner at Hinoki & the Bird, an Asian-inspired restaurant I'd really come to love, and the chef, David Meyers, orchestrated a vegan menu for us. By the end of day two, we were exhausted, and yet we had accomplished something huge: the alignment of an idea. We were on our way to creating a billion dollar lifestyle-brand, and there were no ifs, ands, or buts about it.

But before we could march boldly forward, there were a couple issues to be resolved.

Tamazul had become a dog since we let go of the local favorite chef and replaced him with an outsider . . . never mind that the new chef was Mexican and this was an authentic Mexican concept—the locals wanted the local boy. Sales plummeted and so did morale. By the end of month three, Tamazul was losing $30,000 a month and serving food that was so out of my comfort zone and our company's style, it was not much different than if an environmental rights company was giving away money to the oil and gas industry on a daily basis. We had to stop the bleeding.

I made a decision pretty much on the spot to convert Tamazul to vegan, as I knew Mexican food could be amazing in a vegan context, and it was the path of least resistance. I considered just shutting it down, but taking a $250,000 hit on a recent investment wasn't appetizing at that point. I was certain, with a bit of imagination, we could make it work.

Unfortunately, I had almost no support from the OKC team. The toxic GM quit, leaving her keys in a flower pot outside the restaurant. I offered the Mexican chef the same position in the new concept because he seemed to be talented.

"Sorry, man. Maybe this would work as vegan in Miami or LA, but you should just pack up and leave Oklahoma, man. I'm out, man."

The director was no more help than he'd been the previous weeks when he was running the restaurant into the ground.

"I just don't know how I can get behind plant-based," he said. "It's not what I'm about. Not sure how you can do better than we did."

They were making about three hundred dollars a day, mind you, so I knew we couldn't do much worse.

And poof, we were down a chef, a director, and a GM. What ensued was like a scene from *Planes, Trains, and Automobiles*: the stars seemed to align, and our team hit it out of the park.

Colin Hofer, a GM from M.A.K.E. and a young vegan athlete, jumped on a plane and made his way to Oklahoma. Brittany Williams, one of our admissions coordinators from Seattle, put her aging dog in the back of her car and started driving south. We called Chris Rayman, our former raw food chef from Oklahoma who was still in town, and he called up some colleagues. In five days, Tamazul was cleaned (it needed it badly, despite the kitchen being only ninety days old) and relaunched with a new website, a new menu, and a new staff. Sales were slow, but even from day one, at least we had a purpose and a mission. And it felt great!

Although regulars from our raw food place rejoiced, the community folks weren't all quite as supportive. Namely, the one main food critic, a lumber yard of a man, Dave Cathey (also known as the Food Dude)—who was a friend of our former chef—didn't even bother to see what we were up to.

His column pretty much slammed our mission.

> Yes, veganesque Mexican food is possible. No, it's neither essential nor better. Better for you? Yes. Better for your pocketbook? Not in Kenney's hands. And no, there's very likely no market for it in Oklahoma City.
>
> But Chef Kenney is entitled to attempt to disprove my opinion, and I can say with 100 percent sincerity that I hope he is successful. If he succeeds, I will write about it at length and extol his indomitable spirit. But for now, this is all you're going to read about Tamazul from me . . . [16]

He went on to write about how he'd be back to visit us if we were still open by 2014. Of course, nearly a year later, we were hitting our stride with a chorus of regular fans, and he was nowhere to be found. And why would he be? A man whose livelihood is based on promoting the same heavy, fat-laden foods that make people ill has no vested interest in supporting a vegan place, unless, that is, he saw the light and realized the power of his pen was mightier than the sword. He could simply tell the truth—our vegan cuisine kicked butt; it was ten times better than what was being served before, and you could almost taste our passion in each dish. However, that would be too easy, so the battle must go on.

In addition to our success with the vegan Tamazul, our new book, *Plant Food*, changed the entire landscape of our publishing efforts, with brilliant photography from the talented and crotchety Maine-based Stacey Cramp. Scott's food is so well-suited to print, and Meredith had become an old pro at book production. I was so proud to see this book happen with mostly just moral support and some writing from me.

Our online business became more and more important to me, as it was the most practical way to educate consumers, professionals, and companies about the benefits of a plant-based path. The growth there was so tremendous, it was hard not to let minds run wild—so we didn't even try. The business was working well, but rather than run it as is for a couple years like most practical operators would do, we decided to rebuild the entire thing. "If it ain't broke, don't fix it" didn't apply in our company. Instead, our mantra is "Don't accept it if it can be better." And we had big plans.

The new site would have a community aspect, taking alumni affairs into the next millennium, and a baseline that could support hundreds of classes as we worked with affiliates to broaden the offerings well beyond cooking to all things plants and lifestyle. We had already mostly completed courses in plant-based culinary nutrition, sports nutrition, elite sports nutrition, food photography, and much more.

All this work caught the eye of a financial mastermind in NYC who had recently orchestrated the purchase of Noma, the world's number-one restaurant, located in Copenhagen, Denmark. I got a call, and before I knew it, I was in Denmark meeting the owners and the brilliant young chef, René Redzepi, who I soon realized had more in common with our cuisine than many of our vegan counterparts.

René builds his cuisine around the seasons and the territory, utilizing many of the same contemporary methods and techniques that we employ, and the results are mind blowing. I had to close my eyes for most of the twenty-two courses I enjoyed on one blustery night. I was blown away by my dinner there. I was mesmerized by the vintage potatoes and milk skins, a hauntingly earthy dish as herbal and deep as one can imagine. The wine glasses piled up around our party of ten as we downed oxidized, biodynamic wines, mostly golden and light, with a few sips of local berry liquor at the end.

The meal I'd eaten the evening before at a hot new restaurant, Amass, run by one of René's former chefs, left me similarly satisfied and amazed.

The pumpkin simmered in almond oil at Amass, and the absolutely brilliant vegetable dishes at Noma had reaffirmed the power of my mission. We were part of something incredible, and it wouldn't be long before the world saw that.

After visiting Denmark, the deals continued to flow, so quickly that it required a spreadsheet to keep it all in check. We signed up to do two projects in Merida, Mexico: Datil y Limon, a high-end vegan concept in a beautiful restored home, and D&T Express, a juice bar spin-off down the street. Then we formed a partnership with two dynamic professionals in Calgary, Canada, to launch the region's first cold-pressed juice cleanse business, and we signed a letter of intent to launch a television show in Miami, with the option for others in Paris and Australia. One of our most exciting deals was a lease signing to open M.A.K.E. OUT in Culver City in a gorgeous 2,000-square-foot open space with one of our graduates, Michel Francour, and a cool entrepreneur named Anthony. While all of this movement seems frenetic, it is exactly what our model was built for, a company designed to attract the best opportunities in the plant-based world.

Of course, all this required cash, and we were still burning through it at a rapid pace. Despite growth in many areas of the company, we were still losing money in Oklahoma—not as much, but enough to hurt—and were investing heavily in new projects, online courses, web support, leadership salaries, and all the associated work that goes into building a company.

During this period of enormous growth, I befriended one of the warmest and most dynamic businessmen I've ever known, Sebastiano Castiglioni—"Seba" for short. Seba was kind enough to read our business plan, and after a few months of conversation, he graciously contributed to our brand. There was, however, one substantial glitch just as Seba was about to sign his paperwork to join us. He wrote me:

> *I was looking at the website and ran into The Gothic NE, which features a non-vegetarian menu. I'd like to make sure my participation and investment does not include this restaurant, as I do not invest in any business venture that includes using dead animals in its regular activities.*

This was going to be easier said than done. Even so, I made a decision then and there that The Gothic would also be converted to vegetarian and that our brand would never again be involved in a non-vegetarian concept or business. He was elated; I was stressed; but I believed in this change, even though I knew that The Gothic staff would be unsupportive. I knew that we'd lose some revenue the next summer, but it had to happen. A month later, our company was 100 percent vegetarian and will be for life.

Back in LA, we continued to grow, focusing on the development of three product lines for Whole Foods, participating in events whenever possible, and speaking out, because just making pretty food is never going to be enough. Growing pains ensued, but for the first time in my life, I accepted my role as a team player, mentor, and a leader—not only for my own team, but for all of those passionate souls who visualize a better world, free of animal abuse and the diseases caused by consuming products related to it. I was in for the long haul.

AIRPLANE FOOD

Keep it light. Drink a green juice before and after the flight. Bring a bag of raw macadamia nuts, some chocolate, and plenty of water. If you stay hydrated, you'll be ready to hit the ground running, sans jet-lag.

CRAFTSMAN

Romance is dressed all in black, as usual—boots, long harem pants, jacket, and scarf, all black, wrapped over the top of his head. The gate opens, and he pulls his black Porsche into the garden of a private bed and breakfast on the coast of Belgium, in the city of Knokke.

Romance is Bart Roman, a young Belgian entrepreneur and one of the straightest shooters I've ever met. He's a no-B.S. kind of guy with great instincts and a quietly charming personality. Like so many of our colleagues, he discovered the plant-based lifestyle, found it life-changing, and made it his mission to spread the word. That's how he ended up reaching out to our company and offering to usher me around for three days while we try to finalize our agreement to open a restaurant together in Gent, the city where he lives.

I arrived here only yesterday, landing in Brussels, and Juliana is here with me. These trips are becoming more and more intense; we have a lot to cover in very little time, and we must build relationships and make the right decisions as quickly as possible.

Bart leads us through a wooden doorway into a long room of contemporary but warm furnishings, glowing candles, a beautifully designed open kitchen, and the sound of conversation from twenty-five or so like-minded, artistic, passionate people Bart brought together. Among the group are two of Belgium's most well-known chefs, a talented yoga instructor, a couple artists, the operators of Jus Jus—Belgian's first cold-press juice brand—and several other leaders in their respective fields.

Bart has a big surprise for us. In the kitchen is Laurent de Bremaker, one of our culinary graduates, who now lives in Brussels. He was a great student just a year ago in Santa Monica and has driven to Knokke to prepare ten raw food courses for us. This is what I call a complete moment—seeing one of our students, on the other side of the world, produce a dinner for such a dynamic group. It's indescribable to see our students thread together the vision I first had many years ago.

The topic of conversation is largely plant-based food and its benefits. The major turning point of this year has been how rapidly the acceptance of what we do is spreading and how many informed individuals are informing others about their choices. We are finally, after years of hard work and persistence, at a point where the work we do is recognized internationally, and other passionate groups and individuals are interested in collaborating on new projects. This trip is one of many we've made this year, all taking us a step closer to realizing our mission to change the way the world eats.

• • • • •

A few months earlier, several members of our team were in Hong Kong overseeing a twenty-course, all-raw dinner party for 250 people on the hundredth floor of the ICC Tower, Hong Kong's tallest building. Our Italian partner, Sebastiano, is a noted art dealer, and he hosted this brilliant event at Sky 100, unveiling art valued at more than $200 million. *Tatler Magazine* hosted the event with him, and it was attended by many Asian business, fashion, and society elites, as well as some of the biggest art collectors in the world.

There were five of us there to cater the event: me, Scott, Meredith, Juliana, and Maria, one of our star students from Sweden. My team all arrived earlier in the week and managed the prep with the Ritz team. They also coordinated with Sebastiano's two teams: his art group and his wine experts from Tuscany, who would oversee the beverage aspect.

The Ritz chefs were on point—a literal army of crisp white coats with their German Executive Chef Peter in command. Our cuisine was tight: brilliant red and green oils, edible flowers, perfectly cut crackers and toasts, tiny little dumplings, and the fresh, clean, sensual aroma of raw food. The makeshift kitchen at Suite 100 was reminiscent of a spaceship: rows of meticulously lined plates, all under a soft, bright bluish light.

This was such a far cry from the first raw food event I did at the Puck Building in New York ten years ago. There, we'd served our one-dish repertoire—raw lasagna from a sheet pan—whereas today, we have thousands of beautiful gourmet raw dishes.

We'd already hosted three other large high-profile dinners that year. The first, the South Beach Wine and Food festival, was beautifully curated by our Miami partner, Karla Dascal, who has flawless taste and a brilliant team. We did a similar dinner in New York recently with two other chefs, and another in Miami. Just a few years ago, no one would have considered inviting a vegan brand to such prestigious events.

The travel continues, as well. In addition to Belgium, we are looking at potential projects and partnerships across the globe, including Peru, Sweden, Spain, Greece, Costa Rica, Australia, and at least another dozen. Fortunately, our team loves adventure and meeting new friends, and we are genuinely curious about what is happening with food internationally, so this is a dream come true.

Today, the major chefs all have their eye on plant-based cuisine. They don't always see it as having equal status to traditional foods, but they see it in their side and rearview mirrors. René Redzepi at Noma clearly sees plants as the heart of a meal. The brilliant chef Sergio Herman, of The Jane in Antwerp, also gets it. He gave up his three Michelin stars to develop a couple slightly more casual restaurants, and his are some of the best vegetarian meals I've had. Alain Ducasse, arguably the most well-known chef in the world, recently announced that his namesake restaurant in Paris will now be driven by plant options, and the New York City–based superstar, Jean-Georges Vongerichten, is launching a vegetarian concept any day. The tipping point is nearer than we think.

• • • • •

The night before we leave Belgium, I can't sleep, of course, so I go through a few emails. One catches my eye, a note from a former New York City chef who I haven't heard from in more than a decade. He wrote:

Matthew,

My wife and I had a transcendent and compelling meal at M.A.K.E last night. The food was truly delicious. Your staff is energized and incredibly well informed. It has been a long time. Hope all is well.

I have a another message from a friend in Las Vegas, expressing her desire to see one of Sin City's top chefs do a vegetarian concept, and a note from a yogi from South Africa who has moved to LA and may want to work with us.

In the pitch black of the night, I take a mental snapshot of the progress we've made, how our brand has grown, and how things have blossomed on many levels, but my mind quickly goes to the work we still have to do, to all the moving parts and challenges that will define us—not just today, but far ahead in the future. This job won't be done quite so easily; we still have tall mountains and deep valleys to face.

On the plane the next morning, the full circle of my life washes over me. I'm a few months past my fiftieth birthday, and thanks to green juice, sunshine, and some genetic blessings, I'm as fit and healthy as most thirty-year-olds. My mind is clear and positive, my full head of hair is as thick and brown as it was on a Maine summer afternoon forty-five years ago, and on a personal level, I'm satisfied. Content. I could be happy most any morning that the sun is shining, when the birds are serenading me awake from their palm tree perches at daybreak. I feel happy with the high of a run on the beach or an intense yoga session. I like life to be simple and uncluttered, allowing me plenty of room to be creative.

• • • • •

When I began writing this book, Familius's CEO, Christopher Robbins, expressed his desire for my story and mission to resonate with family values. At the time, I confirmed that it would; food, wellness, nourishment, and other life lessons in this book contribute to personal and family happiness. In reality, though, I knew my track record showed a different theme; I'd often placed other ventures—work, health, travel—before family and relationships.

My fiftieth birthday wasn't as monumental for me as it is for others; I don't have children, I am not married, and I don't feel my age. Rather than party for my birthday, I spent that day—and the weeks before and after it—taking a deeper look at what was most important to me. I love my work and will continue to log what most would consider an extreme amount of weekly hours to my business. But I also had to admit to myself that it was hard to fully enjoy the wonderfully complex business I had built, and the web of global relationships that come with it, if business was my only focus. I'm so fortunate that my parents are doing relatively well and still live in the family home we moved into when I was a year old. And, of course, my cat, Rumple, a beautifully brilliant pet, has been with me every day as I pursue my vision and goals. These relationships bring me joy, and I want to find more time to spend with family and to foster friendships that often are neglected when we're overworked.

During this contemplative period, and when I least expected it, someone special came into my life. Enter Liz Arch, a Los Angeles–based, internationally known yoga teacher, martial artist, writer, and founder of her own brand, Primal Yoga. Liz is talented, gorgeous, extremely intelligent, and incredible to be around, and before I could catch my breath, we were in love. We have the most open communication and the deepest attraction I've ever experienced. Our individual areas of expertise make for the best combination one could ask for in health and wellness, and we both learn from each other.

It took me longer than most to find this harmony in my personal life, but I've always wanted to wait and work for the best life has to offer, and the best things take time. My life has changed. I still focus on my work, but I now have a deep connection to someone who can share my successes and challenges and someone I can support when she needs it.

Christopher will be happy to know that my story embodies the importance of love and family. Without these essential elements, nothing will ever be as meaningful. Love is everything, and it gives me strength and focus to do even better in other areas of my life. The most important thing is to embrace love when it comes into your life; be open to it and don't hold back. You never know exactly where it will take you, but you can only grow from it.

• • • • •

My approach to business these days is broad and bold. I believe in a new future, one where food, all food—whether it is served in hospitals or schools, in fancy restaurants, or at the biggest events in the world, and even food served at home—not only tastes great and looks beautiful but also nourishes those eating it and the planet as a whole. I'm so passionate about this that I'm willing to take major risks, to put my entire well-being on the line to see my vision come to life. Although I'm still not set for life financially, this stopped being about money long ago—aside from striving for the financial freedom to pursue our goals, it was never about money. Money doesn't excite me; change gets my juices flowing. Optimal health excites me. Seeing human and environmental life at its full potential really turns me on, and although food is only one component of global wellness, it's a big component. The food we eat can make a major difference in the well-being of this planet and how we protect its natural resources. In order to make the largest positive impact, we have to think big.

Rather than stop and consider my company's current roster of projects either operating or in development—six restaurants, four on-site culinary academies, an online culinary academy (with a potential licensing deal to produce another for one of the biggest chefs in the world), eleven books, two apps, four calendars, a television show deal, a private chef placement business, and product lines that include a cashew-based ice cream, tree nut cheese, and vegan chocolate . . . oh, and a non-profit, a test kitchen, a few strategic partnerships, and a growing team of about two hundred people—I continue to look for other opportunities to expand our influence.

We have a few projects just ahead, including a new plant-based restaurant that will bring our signature cuisine to my neighborhood in Venice, on the hottest street in America—specifically, Abbot Kinney Boulevard. This deal will open doors to take our brand global. I want to build a foundation that will last, evolve, and become a company powerful enough to reach every major market and bring mind-blowing healthy food to world, and to do it in such an inspiring way that it will change the food paradigm. We need to develop high-profile projects for that vision to be realized.

We have a culinary academy in development in Hua Hin, Thailand; we're opening a vegan restaurant in Mexico; our Miami project is finally on track with construction again; and our fast casual concept, M.A.K.E. OUT, will open around the time this book is published. There are several more online classes in development, and virtually all of our business segments have projects in various stages of development. Our company is not easy to track or easy to manage, but it is easy to say with confidence that we are creating and producing on a daily basis.

With growth comes change, and sometimes challenge. It's been hard to see M.A.K.E., for all its critical acclaim and the gorgeous food it serves, struggling with a modest number of guests each night while Abbot Kinney's mediocre restaurants are jam-packed, so stocked with customers they don't even need to try to be nice. Still, we will keep at it with M.A.K.E. and reevaluate if necessary. Some markets simply aren't ready for us yet.

The road ahead looks pretty good. Still, I've been through enough and am realistic enough to understand that we can only work toward the future; we can't predict it. I'm already satisfied, on many levels, because I know that plant-based cuisine has its foothold and its place in Culinary Art, but I must admit, my desire is ambitious: I'd like to see raw food define culinary art—to be the rule rather than the exception. The environment will benefit tremendously, and I dream of a world where animals will not be subjected to the abuses brought on by factory farming and insensitivity to what we are eating. Food will be more exciting, chefs will be more creative, and the people of this planet will be healthier.

• • • • •

Back in the black car, it's early morning, and Bart is driving me to the airport. I have a new friend, maybe a new restaurant on the way, but more importantly, I have another collaborator to join me on this mission. I have a few green juices next to me and am filling up on liquids before heading to New York to meet Adrian Mueller about a new book. I'm looking forward to an afternoon in Soho and dinner at one of my favorite NYC restaurants, Omen, but I can't wait to get back to LA to see Liz and Rumple.

My career brought such beautiful, brilliant people into my life. If I hadn't made the transition to plants so many years earlier, I can't imagine where I'd be, who I'd be with, or what my future would look like. I'm grateful I had the courage to follow my passion, the strength to persist, and the support of colleagues, family, loved ones, and an open-minded public to allow a vision to become a journey and a reality.

NOTES

1. Gael Green, "Alo Again," *New York Magazine*, August 13, 1990
2. Bryan Miller, "Restaurants," *New York Times*, December 18, 1992
3. Ruth Reichl, "Restaurants," *New York Times*, November 26, 1993
4. Hal Rubenstein, "Canteen," *New York Magazine*, January 24, 2000
5. Gael Greene, "Commune: Matthew Kenney's Commune May Be Scalded by Its Own Heat," *New York Magazine*, May 29, 2000
6. William Grimes, "Restaurants: Bistro Flavors in an Un-bistro-like Setting," *New York Times*, January 2, 2002
7. Matthew Kenney, *Entertaining in the Raw*, Gibbs Smith (2009), p. 11
8. Gael Green, "What Have You Found in the Raw-Food Craze?" *Insatiable Critic*, July 12, 2004
9. Frank Bruni, "Pure Food and Wine," *New York Times*, July 2, 2014
10. Allen Salki, "Into the Fire," *Time Out Magazine*, June 15, 2006
11. Besha Rodell, "M.A.K.E. LIKES IT RAW: And You Might, Too, When You Try Matthew Kenney's Santa Monica Restaurant," *LA Weekly*
12. Jonathan Gold, "Chi Spacca Is All about the Meat," *LA Times*, April 4, 2013
13. Jonathon Gold, "On the M.A.K.E. for Raw Vegan Cuisine," *LA Times*, April 13, 2013
14. Brad Johnson, "No Meat Here, but Perhaps the Most Exquisite Dumplings You'll Ever Experience," *LA Register*, May 7, 2014
15. Gael Greene, "Commune: Matthew Kenney's Commune May Be Scalded by Its Own Heat," *New York Magazine*, May 29, 2000
16. Dave Cathey, "Nic's Expands Brand, Tamazul Shrinks Its Potential Audience, and Other Nuggets Heard on the Line," *The Oklahoman*, October 17, 2013

ABOUT THE AUTHOR

MATTHEW KENNEY is an American celebrity chef, author, speaker, educator, and entrepreneur specializing in plant-based food. He has authored 11 books and is the founder of Matthew Kenney Cuisine, an integrated lifestyle company as well as the Matthew Kenney Culinary Academy, a raw food education center offering courses online; in Santa Monica, California; Belfast, Maine; Miami, Florida; and Hua Hin, Thailand. He lives in Venice, California.

ABOUT FAMILIUS

VISIT OUR WEBSITE: WWW.FAMILIUS.COM

Our website is a different kind of place. Get inspired, read articles, discover books, watch videos, connect with our family experts, download books and apps and audiobooks, and along the way, discover how values and happy family life go together.

JOIN OUR FAMILY

There are lots of ways to connect with us! Subscribe to our newsletters at www.familius.com to receive uplifting daily inspiration, essays from our Pater Familius, a free ebook every month, and the first word on special discounts and Familius news.

BECOME AN EXPERT

Familius authors and other established writers interested in helping families be happy are invited to join our family and contribute online content. If you have something important to say on the family, join our expert community by applying at:
www.familius.com/apply-to-become-a-familius-expert

GET BULK DISCOUNTS

If you feel a few friends and family might benefit from what you've read, let us know and we'll be happy to provide you with quantity discounts. Simply email us at specialorders@familius.com.

Website: www.familius.com
Facebook: www.facebook.com/paterfamilius
Twitter: @familiustalk, @paterfamilius1
Pinterest: www.pinterest.com/familius

The most important work
you ever do will be within the
walls of your own home.